Smartphones, Current Events, and Mobile Information Behavior

Smartphones, Current Events, and Mobile Information Behavior provides unprecedented insights into young people's news consumption patterns and the ecology of mobile news. Advancing our knowledge of mobile behavior, the book also highlights the ways in which mobile news impacts the lives of the general public.

Using a multi-faceted research model on mobile news consumption behavior, Oh and Tang examined a wide spectrum of mobile news consumption activities, outlined the key characteristics of mobile news, as well as captured users' near real-time evaluation of and emotional reactions to news stories. The book also shows that the process of using smartphones to receive, read, find, share, and store news stories has resulted in new behavioral patterns that enable people to consume news in a multifaceted way. Analyzing the extent and various methods of mobile news sharing can, Oh and Tang argue, help us understand how such exchanges reshape contemporary society. Demonstrating that mobile news consumption is now an integral part of people's daily lives, the book clearly shows that its impact on people's day-to-day activities, and their political and social lives cannot be underestimated.

Smartphones, Current Events, and Mobile Information Behavior will be useful to scholars, students, and practitioners who are studying library and information science, journalism and media, digital communication, user behavior, information technology, human-computer interaction, marketing, political science, psychology, and sociology.

Kyong Eun Oh is Associate Professor and the Co-Director of the Ph.D. program in the School of Library and Information Science at Simmons University. Her research interests include personal information management, information behavior including mobile news information behavior, and information organization. She studies how people manage and organize their digital files and how people use and interact with information in everyday life.

Rong Tang is Full Professor and the Co-Director of the Ph.D. program at the School of Library and Information Science at Simmons University. She is Co-Leader for the Research Data Management Librarian Academy (RDMLA) and for the Data Services Continuing Professional Education (DSCPE) program. Professionally, Tang serves as the President for Association for Library and Information Science Education (ALISE) 2022–2023. Her research interests include mobile news information behavior, research data management services, open government data, usability and user experience, social support during the pandemic, and paradigm shift in the field of information.

Smartphones, Current Events, and Mobile Information Behavior

Consuming, Reacting, Sharing, and Connecting through News

Kyong Eun Oh and Rong Tang

Routledge
Taylor & Francis Group
LONDON AND NEW YORK

First published 2024
by Routledge
4 Park Square, Milton Park, Abingdon, Oxon OX14 4RN

and by Routledge
605 Third Avenue, New York, NY 10158

Routledge is an imprint of the Taylor & Francis Group, an informa business

British Library Cataloguing-in-Publication Data
A catalogue record for this book is available from the British Library

ISBN: 978-0-367-51207-1 (hbk)
ISBN: 978-0-367-51241-5 (pbk)
ISBN: 978-1-003-05300-2 (ebk)

DOI: 10.4324/9781003053002

Typeset in Times New Roman
by Newgen Publishing UK

Contents

List of figures *xi*
List of tables *xiii*

1 Background and Introduction 1
1.1 Overview of the role of mobile devices in news consumption 1
1.2 Global trends and worldwide mobile news consumption 2
1.3 Empirical studies on mobile news consumption 3
1.3.1 News consumer typology and news consumption frameworks 4
1.3.2 Empirical studies on mobile news consumption 6
1.4 Background and introduction of the present research 8
1.4.1 Historical and political context 8
1.4.2 Overview of the research work 9
1.5 Research model for mobile news consumption behavior 11

2 Mobile News Consumed by Study Participants 14
2.1 Study participants 14
2.1.1 Pre-diary survey participants 14
2.1.2 Diary study participants 14
2.1.3 Follow-up interview participants 16
2.2 Types of news 16
2.3 Sources of news 18
2.4 Formats of news 19
2.5 Demographic differences 21
2.5.1 Demographics and the types of news 21

2.5.2 Demographic differences in the sources of news 24
2.5.3 Demographic differences in the formats of news 27
2.6 Summary 29

3 Mobile News Consumption Cycle and Activities 31
3.1 Receiving/noticing news 31
3.1.1 Reasons for receiving/noticing news items 32
3.1.1.1 Gender 32
3.1.1.2 Age group 33
3.1.1.2 Classes 33
3.1.1.3 Majors or academic specializations 35
3.1.1.4 Additional reasons for noticing news 36
3.1.2 Parts of news stories drawing people's attention 37
3.1.2.1 Gender 37
3.1.2.2 Classes 38
3.1.2.3 Majors 39
3.2 Reading news 40
3.2.1 News reading behavior 40
3.2.1.1 Demographic differences 41
3.2.2 Methods of reading 41
3.2.2.1 Overall methods of reading 41
3.2.2.2 Demographic differences in reading methods 42
3.2.3 Additional insights about reading behavior and methods 44
3.2.3.1 Reading behavior 45
3.2.3.2 Reasons for reading or not reading mobile news 46
3.2.3.3 Reading methods 46
3.3 Finding news 46
3.3.1 News finding behavior 49
3.3.1.1 Demographic differences 49
3.3.2 Methods of finding the news 50
3.3.2.1 Age group 51
3.3.2.2 Ethnicity 52
3.3.2.3 Class 53
3.3.2.4 Major 54
3.3.3 Additional insights about finding behavior and methods 55

3.3.3.1 News finding behavior or methods 55
3.3.3.2 Reasons for finding news 56
3.4 Sharing news 57
3.4.1 News sharing behaviors 57
3.4.1.1 Age groups 57
3.4.1.2 Ethnicity 57
3.4.1.3 School types 57
3.4.1.4 Classes 58
3.4.1.5 Student types 58
3.4.2 Methods of news sharing 58
3.4.2.1 Overview of news sharing methods 58
3.4.2.2 Demographic differences in news sharing methods 58
3.4.3 The extent of news sharing 61
3.4.3.1 Overview of the extent of news sharing 61
3.4.3.2 Demographic differences in the extent of sharing 62
3.4.4 Additional insights about sharing behavior and methods 64
3.4.4.1 News sharing behavior 64
3.4.4.2 Reasons for sharing or not sharing news 65
3.4.4.3 News sharing methods 67
3.4.4.4 Reasons for choosing a news sharing method 68
3.5 Storing news 69
3.5.1 News storing behaviors 69
3.5.2 Demographic differences in how to store news 70
3.5.2.1 Gender 70
3.5.2.2 Age group 71
3.5.2.3 Ethnicity 72
3.5.2.4 School types 73
3.5.2.5 Class 74
3.5.2.6 Major 74
3.5.3 Additional insights about storing behavior and methods 76
3.5.3.1 Regular news storing behavior 76
3.5.3.2 Reasons for storing news items 77
3.6 Summary 77

4 Mobile News Reactions: Evaluative Reactions, Affective Reactions 79

4.1 Use of semantic differential scales for gauging people's evaluative and affective reactions to news 79

4.1.1 Bipolar adjective pairs for evaluative reactions 80

4.1.2 Bipolar adjective pairs for affective reactions 80

4.2 Evaluative reactions 81

4.2.1 Evaluative reactions to news 81

4.2.2 Variations of evaluative reactions by types of news 81

4.2.2.1 Deep vs shallow 82

4.2.2.2 Valuable vs worthless 82

4.2.2.3 Heavy vs light 82

4.2.2.4 Sharp vs dull 83

4.2.2.5 Honest vs dishonest 83

4.2.2.6 Fresh vs stale 83

4.2.2.7 Beneficial vs harmful 84

4.2.2.8 Beautiful vs ugly 84

4.2.2.9 Good vs bad 84

4.2.3 Variations of evaluative reactions by demographic attributes 84

4.3 Affective reactions 87

4.3.1 Affective reactions to news 87

4.3.2 Variations of affective reactions by types of news 88

4.3.2.1 Strong vs weak 88

4.3.2.2 Calm vs agitated 88

4.3.2.3 Pleasant vs unpleasant 89

4.3.2.4 Happy vs sad 89

4.3.2.5 Peaceful vs ferocious 89

4.3.2.6 Relaxed vs tense 90

4.3.2.7 Nice vs awful 90

4.3.2.8 Bright vs dark 90

4.3.2.9 Smooth vs rough 90

4.3.2.10 Comfortable vs uncomfortable 91

4.3.2.11 Pleasurable vs painful 91

4.3.3 Variations of affective reactions by demographic attributes 91

4.4 Further observation of evaluative and affective reactions to news based on follow-up interviews 92

4.4.1 *Further investigation of evaluative reactions to news 92*
4.4.1.1 *Deep vs shallow 92*
4.4.1.2 *Valuable vs worthless 93*
4.4.1.3 *Honest vs dishonest 95*
4.4.1.4 *Fresh vs stale 95*
4.4.1.5 *Fair vs unfair 95*
4.4.1.6 *Beneficial vs harmful 96*
4.4.1.7 *Beautiful vs ugly 96*
4.4.1.8 *Good vs bad 96*
4.4.2 *Further investigation of affective reactions to news 96*
4.4.2.1 *Strong vs weak 96*
4.4.2.2 *Calm vs agitated 98*
4.4.2.3 *Happy vs sad 98*
4.4.2.4 *Relaxed vs tense 99*
4.4.2.5 *Bright vs dark 99*
4.4.3 *Further investigation of conflicting reactions to news 100*
4.4.3.1 *Valuable vs shallow 100*
4.4.3.2 *Beneficial vs ugly 101*
4.4.3.3 *Beautiful vs harmful 101*
4.4.3.4 *Fresh vs dull 102*
4.4.3.5 *Honest vs unfair 102*
4.4.3.6 *Good vs unpleasant 103*
4.4.3.7 *Pleasurable vs uncomfortable 103*
4.4.3.7 *Sets of conflicting reactions 104*
4.5 *Summary 105*

5 Summary and Conclusion 107
5.1 *Overview 107*
5.2 *Impact on mobile activities, social behavior, and political/community engagement 107*
5.2.1 *Political and society news examples 109*
5.2.2 *Entertainment news examples 110*
5.2.3 *Sports news examples 114*
5.2.4 *Science/technology news examples 114*
5.2.5 *Public health or health news examples 117*
5.2.6 *Other types of news examples 121*

5.3 Recommendations on mobile device and news app design 123
5.4 Further areas of exploration and examination 125
5.5 Summary 125

Index 127

Figures

1.1 Research Model for Mobile News Consumption Behavior 12
2.1 Types of News Consumption by Participants 18
2.2 Sources of News Consumed by Participants 20
2.3 Formats of News Consumed by Participants 21
3.1 Parts of the News Used by Participants in Noticing the News Items 38
5.1 Muslim Women Call out Donald Trump 110
5.2 Munich Shooting News 111
5.3 Wikileaks and Sanders versus Clinton 111
5.4 The Racist History of Portland 112
5.5 Pokémon Sun and Moon Game 112
5.6 Netflix's "Little Witch Academia" Trailer 113
5.7 Feud between Taylor Swift and Kim Kardashian/ Kanye West 113
5.8 Katie Ledecky Broke the World Record and Got the First Gold Medal for the United States 114
5.9 Russian Team Banned from Olympics 115
5.10 Ramp for Competitors' Boats Collapsed 115
5.11 Australia Refused to Move Their Team to the Olympic Village 116
5.12 Skydiver with No Parachute 116
5.13 Europe's First Mars Rover 117
5.14 Solar-powered Plane 118
5.15 FishFace Technology 118
5.16 Smartphone Technology 119
5.17 Zika Virus 119

5.18 Zika Virus and Impact on Pregnant Women 120
5.19 Deep Space and Heart Problems 120
5.20 Depression and Sadness 121
5.21 Yahoo to Sell Web Business to Verizon 122
5.22 More Is Better: Fitness Advice 122
5.23 Friends and You 123

Tables

1.1	Types of News Consumers, Their Age Groups, and the Important or Low Important Sources of News	5
1.2	Data Collection Methods and the Timeline	9
2.1	Formal Survey Respondents' Demographic Information	15
2.2	Diary Study Respondents' Demographic Information	15
2.3	Interviewees' Demographic Information	17
2.4	Top Three Types of News Consumed by Participants in Different Age Groups	22
2.5	Top Three Types of News Consumed by Participants in Different Majors	23
2.6	Top Three Types of News Consumed by Undergraduate and Graduate Participants	23
2.7	Top Three Sources of News Consumed by Participants in Different Age Groups	24
2.8	Top Three Sources of News Consumed by Undergraduate and Graduate Participants	24
2.9	Top Three Sources of News Consumed by Participants in Different Ethnicities	25
2.10	Top Three Sources of News Consumed by Participants in Different Majors	25
2.11	Top Three Formats of News Consumed by Participants in Different Age Groups	27
2.12	Top Three Formats of News Consumed by Participants in Different Majors	28
2.13	Top Three Formats of News Consumed by Participants in Different Ethnicities	29

3.1	Reasons for Participants to Notice or Receive News from Mobile Devices	32
3.2	Top 3 Reasons for Participants of Various Age Groups to Notice or Receive News from Mobile Devices	33
3.3	Top 3 Reasons for Participants of Various Classes to Notice or Receive News from Mobile Devices	34
3.4	Top 3 Reasons for Participants of Various Majors to Notice or Receive News from Mobile Devices	35
3.5	Top 3 Sections of the News Stories that Drew Participants of Various Class Levels' Attention	39
3.6	Top 3 Sections that Participant of Various Majors Noticed When Receiving News from Mobile Devices	40
3.7	Participants' Reading Behavior	42
3.8	Top 3 Methods of Reading by Majors	44
3.9	Common Reasons for Reading or Not Reading News	47
3.10	Reasons for Using a Method of Reading News	48
3.11	Participants' Finding Behavior	49
3.12	Top 3 News Finding Methods by Age Groups	51
3.13	Top 3 News Finding Methods by Ethnic Groups	52
3.14	Top 3 News Finding Methods by Class Levels	53
3.15	Top 3 News Finding Methods by Majors	55
3.16	Participants' News Sharing Methods	59
3.17	Top 3 News Sharing Methods by Gender	59
3.18	Top 3 News Sharing Methods by Ethnic Groups	60
3.19	Top 3 News Sharing Methods by Major Groups	61
3.20	Reasons for Sharing or Not Sharing News	65
3.21	Participants' News Storing Methods	70
3.22	Participants' Top News Storing Methods by Gender	71
3.23	Participants' Top News Storing Methods by Age Groups	72
3.24	Participants' Top News Storing Methods by Ethnic Groups	73
3.25	Participants' Top News Storing Methods by School Types	74
3.26	Participants' Top News Storing Methods by Class Levels	75
3.27	Participants' Top News Storing Methods by Majors	76
4.1	Adjective Pairs for Evaluative Reactions	80
4.2	Adjective Pairs for Affective Reactions	81

1 Background and Introduction

1.1 Overview of the role of mobile devices in news consumption

With the widespread use of mobile devices in our daily life, more and more people rely on their smartphones to consume news. In their Digital News Report 2019, based on their survey data "from almost 40 countries and six continents," Newman, Fletcher, Kalogeropoulos, and Nielsen (2019) indicated, "The smartphone continues to grow in importance for news, with two-thirds (66%) now using the device to access news weekly (+4pp) (p. 10)." According to the same report, there are age differences as well as differences between types of users in the use of smartphones for news consumption. Specifically, a higher proportion of younger users use mobile phones for news frequently,

> Nearly half of Gen Z news users (45%) in our combined sample come into first contact with news in the morning via the smartphone, with only 19% via TV and 5% via desktops/laptops. Similar trends can be seen among Gen Y, who also first turn to their smartphone (39%) over TV (22%) or the computer (8%). By a sharp contrast, for over 35s television is still the most likely first contact point with news (30%), with smartphone (19%) and radio (18%) some way behind.
>
> (Newman et al., 2019, p. 54)

Furthermore, the report reveals that "Heavy news users are 2.5 times more likely to use mobile alerts than casual news users" (p. 14). Newman et al. further indicate that

> Smartphone sales may be slowing down but the previous section shows how our dependence on them for news continues to grow. Two-thirds of our combined sample (66%) now uses

DOI: 10.4324/9781003053002-1

> the smartphone for news weekly, with usage doubling in most countries over the last seven years.
>
> (p. 16)

From the point of view of the flow of news production, Sheller (2015) indicated the transformational power of mobile interfaces. She pointed out, "News production, distribution, and consumption has been transformed by new mobile interfaces, at first simply due to the digital delivery of content to internet platforms, but now especially by the proliferation of those that are socially connected and interactive" (p. 15). It is undeniable that mobile phones have become one of the primary tools for our daily news consumption.

There are multiple significant factors that motivated us to work on this book. First and foremost, the general public's interactive and participatory process of news consumption, enabled by smartphone technology and news app functions, is known only a little through a number of existing empirical studies on the subject. The depth of which, i.e., how this process has fundamentally altered the nature of news consumption, and how the mobile-native generation evaluates and emotionally reacts to the news, is seldom examined. Through this book, we examine a wide spectrum of mobile news consumption activities, with rich data on people's behavior, their near real-time assessments of and emotional reactions to news stories. Moreover, we attempt to provide unprecedented insights into young people's news consumption patterns and the ecosystem of mobile news. Second, understanding the contemporary mobile news ecosystem also helps to identify gaps in mobile technology development, which will generate ideas for mobile news app developers to improve their apps to better facilitate a seamless interaction within mobile news ecosystems. Finally, as a social phenomenon, the co-consumption and socialization aspects of mobile news sharing, commenting, screenshots, or links exchanging are worthwhile to examine, as they help us understand how such exchanges redefined contemporary society. Studying the social aspects of mobile news consumption also helps us capture emergent social variables, which play a predominant role in people's daily lives.

1.2 Global trends and worldwide mobile news consumption

The popularity of using a smartphone to access news is not only a trend in the United States but also in many other countries.

Newman et al. (2019) reported that 28% of people in the United Kingdom regard the smartphone as the main gateway to the news, which was higher than TV (27%). In addition, 43% of mobile phone users in the United Kingdom indicated that when they use a smartphone, they first go to a news website or app (p. 15). In China, 64% of users reported that they read news via their mobile phones at least once a day, and 90% of users read news through their mobile phones at least once a week (Deloitte, 2018, p. 11). An interesting trend of mobile phone users in China is that video news content has become an increasingly critical source of information. Deloitte (2018) reported that 54% of Chinese mobile phone users watched video news at least once a day, which was much higher than the global average (21%).

Consuming news via mobile phones involves various activities such as receiving news, finding news, and sharing news. Previous reports showed that smartphones are an essential part of different news consumption activities in many countries. More specifically, according to Silver et al. (2019), the majority of mobile users in Kenya (88%), Philippines (85%), South Africa (85%), Venezuela (83%), India (81%), Columbia (79%), Jordan (78%), Lebanon (77%), Tunisia (75%), Mexico (74%), and Vietnam (87%) responded that their mobile phones helped them obtain information and news about important issues (pp. 37–38). In terms of finding news, Newman et al. (2019) reported that "Yahoo! News reaches two-thirds (66%) of mobile phone users in Japan each week, Naver reaches 73% of smartphone users in South Korea, while Line Today reaches 47% of Taiwanese participants" (p. 17), showing that it is one of the primary mobile news consumption behaviors in Asian countries. In the case of sharing news, Newman et al. reported that 53% of participants in Brazil, 50% of respondents in Malaysia, and 49% of participants in South Africa used WhatsApp for discussing and sharing news (p. 9).

1.3 Empirical studies on mobile news consumption

There have been many published empirical studies that are relevant to the understanding of mobile news consumption. These publications can be grouped into three themes: (1) Theories or conceptual models on news consumption in a digital environment, (2) studies on mobile news consumption within specific countries or a comparative international scope, and (3) mobile news production and consumption from a journalism point of view.

1.3.1 News consumer typology and news consumption frameworks

With the emergence of digital news media, there is a range of reports/publications investigating the characteristics of news consumers. For example, Pew Research Center (2008) conducted the 2008 biennial news consumption survey that involved more than 3,600 people nationwide within the United States and discovered that there were four segments of news consumers: Traditionalists, Integrators, Net-Newsers, and Disengaged. While Traditionalists were the oldest and largest news segment, Integrators were the second largest segment who were middle-aged, educated, and affluent. Traditionalists get news from television or other traditional media sources almost exclusively and "rarely go online for news" (p. 47). Integrators obtained their news from both traditional sources such as TV and the internet. Compared to other news consumer groups, Integrators "spend more time with the news on a typical day than do those who rely more on either traditional or internet sources; far more enjoy keeping up with the news a lot than in any other news segment." Net-Newsers were the youngest news user group with a median age of 35. Net-Newsers relied "primarily on the internet for news, they are leading the way in using new web features and other technologies." Finally, the fourth group "the Disengaged," consisting of 14% of the public, were bystanders of news consumption. They "do not closely follow any of the following: local, national, international, or business and finance news" (p. 47).

In 2010, Schroder and Kobbernagel (2010) conducted a qualitative Q method study involving 35 participants as Danish cross-media news consumers and categorized the news consumer segments into seven groups: (1) The traditional, versatile news consumer, (2) the popular culture-oriented digital news consumer, (3) the background-oriented digital news consumer, (4) the light newspaper reader, (5) the heavy newspaper reader, (6) the news update addict, and (7) the regional omnivorous news consumer. Table 1.1 summarizes the types of news consumers, their age groups, and the important or less important sources of news.

The news consumption topologies presented by both the Pew Research Center and Schroder and Kobbernagel (2010) highlight

Table 1.1 Types of News Consumers, Their Age Groups, and the Important or Low Important Sources of News

News Consumers	*Demographic Characteristics*	*Important Media Sources*	*Less Important Media Sources*
The traditional, versatile news consumer	College educated, older than 35–40	• National newspapers • Serious current affairs TV programs • Primetime TV news • Radio morning news • Net-based news services	• Mobile phone news • Blogs with news • Tabloid newspapers
The popular culture-oriented digital news consumer	Not yet have college degrees, in their 20s	• Net-based media	• Serious current affairs TV programs • International TV news and current affairs • International net news
The background-oriented digital news consumer	Live in Copenhagen 20s	• Net-based news • Mobile news	• Entertaining TV current affairs programs • Weekly magazines
The light newspaper reader	Male, no college degree, live in Copenhagen	• Primetime TV news and net-based news • Tabloid newspapers and free	• Professional magazines • International non-media news sites • National niche newspapers
The heavy newspaper reader	College educated, over 60s	• Newspapers (national newspapers, specialized newspapers) • Local weeklies • Free newspapers • Primetime TV news and net-based news	• News blogs • Morning radio news • Mobile phone news • Weekly magazines • Current affairs TV

(*Continued*)

Table 1.1 (Continued)

News Consumers	*Demographic Characteristics*	*Important Media Sources*	*Less Important Media Sources*
The news update addict	No college degree or bachelor's degree, male, under 40 years of age	• 24-hour TV news • Text-TV • Mobile phone news	• News blogs • Radio current affairs • International non-media news sites
The regional omnivorous news consumer	Live in a provincial town, have less education than a master's degree from university	• Regional dailies • Serious and entertaining TV current affairs programs • Weekly magazines • Professional magazines	• International non-media news sites • News blogs • International news media websites

the penetration of net-based news and mobile phone news to digital news consumers. In Schroder and Kobbernagel's (2010) more detailed grouping of news consumers, net-based media was the top media source for six groups, whereas mobile phone news occurred in two groups. Now that more than 10 years have passed since Schroder and Kobbernagel's (2010) publication, the use of mobile phones and consuming news via smartphones is more permanent. As reported by Newman et al., "The smartphone continues to grow in importance for news, with two-thirds (66%) now using the device to access news weekly (+4pp)" (2019, p. 10).

1.3.2 Empirical studies on mobile news consumption

Multiple empirical studies (e.g., Van Damme, Courtois, Verbrugge, & De Marez, 2015; Westlund, 2008) focused specifically on mobile news consumption and the use of mobile news services. Van Damme et al. (2015) defined mobile news consumption as "rather news consumption on a mobile device than 'mobile' news, since domestic news consumption exceeds the mobile news consultation throughout the day" (p. 206). In their study of media consumption, Taneja, Webster, and Malthouse (2012) observed two rounds of participants (n = 495, round 1; n = 476 round 2) in terms of their media consumption activities. In both rounds of observation, four factors were extracted, with the "Television Viewing" factor containing the element of "news program" and the "Media Online" factor consisting of the element of "Web news and sports." The authors explained the third factor, "Media on mobile," repertoire as such: it

> combines the different uses of mobile phones. Mobile talk and text messaging are platforms with the highest loadings on this factor followed by internet access on mobile phones. Another item with a strong loading is "mobile other," which captures the use of a mobile phone as a camera, camcorder, and voice recorder.
>
> (p. 960)

Even though this research did not focus on mobile media consumption from the perspective of mobile news consumption, its findings related to media consumption patterns, individual characteristics such as age and educational backgrounds, how users rely on habit and interaction, and how gratification theories may influence users' preferences of media consumptions shed light on the understanding of mobile news consumption.

In another study, Westlund (2008) reported results of multiple SOM (Society, Opinion and Media) national surveys from 2005, 2006, and 2007 in Sweden, and found that

> Frequent usage of mobile news services is associated with two particular lifestyles. The first is associated with being on the go: usage is higher among people who often engage themselves in activities outside their homes, such as going to pubs and restaurants. The second lifestyle dimension is related to work: people who often work overtime and travel in their work are overrepresented as mobile news users.
>
> (Westlund, 2008, p. 452)

Westlund (2008) observes that

> The mobile device is becoming a supplementary news medium to other news media predominantly among specific user groups. These people are always connected and appreciate access to news independent of time and space. The mobile device is

> improving people's ability to receive news about current events in the world.
>
> (Westlund, 2008, p. 460)

Seven years later, Jansson and Lindell (2015) also analyzed the SOM survey in Sweden, this time on 2010 data, and contested that "What we are witnessing is thus more than a technological and representational transition; it is a multi-layered spatial transition that can be described as a shift from *mass media textures* to *transmedia textures*" (p. 80). Jansson and Lindell found that mobile news consumption had significant correlations with both work-related international mobility and leisure-related international mobility. Jansson and Lindell (2015) concluded that "We are witnessing a paradigmatic transition as to the ways in which news is consumed; the spatial practice of news consumption is changing into an increasingly amalgamated, mobile practice" (p. 92).

In summary, with the advancement of mobile technology affording the ability to consume news on smartphones, multiple studies examined the types of news consumers, including those inclined to consume news on mobile devices. The empirical studies in this area revealed not only that mobile devices can be a supplementary news consumption tool but that they actually represent a fundamental paradigm shift – mobile news consumption has become an everyday news consumption practice that increasingly replaces the conventional spatially oriented news consumption practice.

1.4 Background and introduction of the present research

1.4.1 Historical and political context

In the summer and fall of 2016, a number of news stories were released relating to two big, contemporaneous events: the 2016 Rio Summer Olympics that took place in Brazil from August 5 to August 21, and the 2016 United States presidential election that was held on November 8. Other major events that happened in the summer and fall of 2016 included a Zika virus outbreak; the Syrian civil war; Brexit; the coup in Turkey; mass shootings and multiple terror attacks in different parts of the world, including Orlando in Florida, Dallas in Texas, and Nice in France; the release of the augmented reality mobile game Pokémon GO; an earthquake in central Italy; North Korea's missile and nuclear tests; and NASA's launch of OSIRS-REx. Since our study investigated how people process and react to news, collected data in our study were inevitably affected by the historical and political context of the time.

1.4.2 Overview of the research work

Our research work on mobile news consumption was initiated in an effort to understand mobile news information behavior among university students in the United States. In particular, we wanted to use a specific period in time, that is, summer and early fall of 2016, as a window to investigate the everyday behavior and natural activities of news consumers on smartphones, and this included the general characteristics such as the types, formats, and sources of the news they consume, various activities related to news consumption such as receiving, reading, finding, sharing, and storing news via their mobile phones, and how people react to news items evaluatively and emotionally.

Through a series of research activities, we gathered data by using multiple data collection methods in order to capture a full range of consumption activities and various aspects of mobile news information behavior. Table 1.2 displays the data collection methods, the timeline, and the number of participants who participated in each data collection stage.

First, the screener survey was sent out to recruit participants who were eligible for the project. It asked whether the respondents owned a smartphone, whether they routinely used their

Table 1.2 Data Collection Methods and the Timeline

Data Collection Methods	*Data Collection Periods*	*Number of Participants*
Participant screener survey	June–October, 2016	111
Pre-diary online survey	June–October, 2016	63
Mobile diary study	July–October, 2016	51
Follow-up interview	August–November, 2016	15

smartphone to receive, read, find, or share news, and brief demographic questions. If the respondents selected "no" to the first two questions, they were asked to exit the survey.

Second, based on the screener survey responses, we invited the qualified respondents (i.e., those who selected "yes" to the first two questions in the screener survey) to participate in a pre-diary online survey. This survey was designed to collect some comprehensive information on participants' news processing behavior in general. The pre-diary online survey asked their news behavior (e.g., types of news they follow, primary media to process news); smartphone and its use (e.g., brand/model, year of use); mobile news behavior (e.g., frequency and proficiency of processing mobile news, satisfaction in processing mobile news, types of apps to process news); and demographic information (e.g., age, gender, ethnicity, nationality, school, major). In addition, participants were asked to indicate their interest in participating in the post-diary follow-up interview.

Third, participants were asked to start a three-week mobile diary study by downloading the mobile diary app, FlexMR, on their smartphones and entering a diary entry each time they processed a news item. They were asked to submit up to 12 news items that they read through their mobile phones, which would mean entering 12 diary entries. Each diary entry asked them to report the title of the news item, format of the news item, how they learned about this news item, primary reasons for noticing the news item, activities they performed with the news item, details about each activity they performed, and any further comments about how they dealt with the news item. There was also an option to upload a screenshot of the news item. In addition, 11 evaluative semantic differential pairs and 12 emotional semantic differential pairs were provided to report their various evaluative and emotional reactions to each news item.

Lastly, we contacted participants of the diary study who indicated interest in participating in the follow-up interview based on the pre-diary online survey response. The follow-up interview questions were tailored to each participant to elicit a richer and more in-depth exploration of their specific mobile news action as reported through their diary entries.

Through multiple points of data collection, we were able to obtain valuable information about the characteristics of mobile news that are consumed by participants such as the types of news and formats of news people consume via their smartphones, where they get news, and whether people with different demographic characteristics consume news differently. We could also learn in-depth about how people receive news, read news, find news, share news, and store news by using their smartphones. It was also very interesting to see how people reacted to each news item, and sometimes even showed some contradictory reactions. In addition, we could take a closer look at individual cases, i.e., how different people consumed, reacted, shared, and connected through news. The details of our findings are shared in the following chapters of this book.

1.5 Research model for mobile news consumption behavior

In our series of investigations, we studied multiple facets of news consumption behavior. At the base level, we examined different characteristics of news consumed by our participants, including the types of news they consumed (e.g., political news, sports news); the sources of news (e.g., news apps, social media); as well as the format of news (e.g., text, image, video, etc.). We also took into account the demographic attributes of our participants, including gender, age group, ethnicity, and more. The core areas of our investigation were (1) specific news consumption activities during the consumption lifecycle, moving from noticing or receiving news, to finding news, to reading news, to sharing news, and to storing news and (2) reactions to news, including evaluative reactions and affective (emotional) reactions. We found that participants' demographic attributes impact on individual news consumption activities as well as participants' reactions to the news. The characteristics of news also impact on the news consumption activities as well as participants' reactions to the news.

Our research model (see Figure 1.1), consequently, consists of four areas, with news consumption activities as the primary core, and reactions to the news as the secondary core, whereas both participants' demographic attributes and characteristics of news impact on both cores.

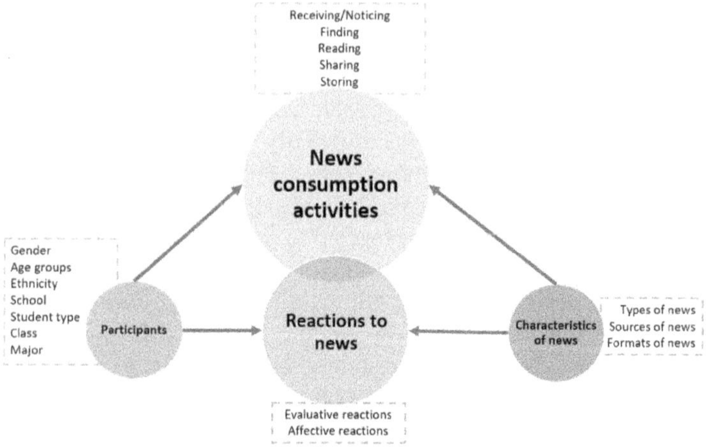

Figure 1.1 Research Model for Mobile News Consumption Behavior.

References

Deloitte (2018). *China mobile consumer survey*. Rctrieved from www2.deloitte.com/content/dam/Deloitte/cn/Documents/technology-media-telecommunications/deloitte-cn-2018-mobile-consumer-survey-en-190121.pdf

Jansson, A., & Lindell, J. (2015). News media consumption in the transmedia age. *Journalism Studies, 16*(1), 79–96. https://doi.org/10.1080/1461670X.2014.890337

Newman, N., Fletcher, R., Kalogeropoulos, A., & Nielsen, R. K. (2019). *Reuters institute digital news report 2019*. Retrieved from https://reutersinstitute.politics.ox.ac.uk/sites/default/files/2019-06/DNR_2019_FINAL_0.pdf

Pew Research Center. (2008). *Key news audiences now blend online and traditional sources*. Retrieved from www.pewresearch.org/politics/2008/08/17/key-news-audiences-now-blend-online-and-traditional-sources/

Schroder, K. C., & Kobbernagel, C. (2010). Towards a typology of cross-media news consumption: A qualitative quantitative synthesis. *Northern Lights: Film and Media Studies Yearbook, 8*(1), 115–137. https://doi.org/10.1386/nl.8.115_1

Sheller, M. (2015). News now. *Journalism Studies, 16*(1), 12–26. https://doi.org/10.1080/1461670X.2014.890324

Silver, L., Smith, A., Johnson, C., Taylor, K., Jiang, J., Anderson, M., & Rainie, L. (2019). *Mobile connectivity in emerging economies*. Pew

Research Center. www.pewresearch.org/internet/2019/03/07/mobile-connectivity-in-emerging-economies/

Taneja, H., Webster, J. G., Malthouse, E. C., & Ksiazek, T. B. (2012). Media consumption across platforms: Identifying user-defined repertoires. *New Media & Society*, *14*(6), 951–968. https://doi.org/10.1177/1461444811436146

Van Damme, K., Courtois, C., Verbrugge, K., & De Marez, L. (2015). What's APPening to news? A mixed-method audience-centred study on mobile news consumption. *Mobile Media & Communication, 3*(2), 196–213. https://doi.org/10.1177/2050157914557691

Westlund, O. (2008). From mobile phone to mobile device: News consumption on the go. *Canadian Journal of Communication, 33*(3), 443–463. https://doi.org/10.22230/cjc.2008v33n3a2004

2 Mobile News Consumed by Study Participants

Through the diary study portion of our project, mobile consumption behavior was reported for 522 news items. Based on the analysis of those news items, information regarding the types of news people consume (e.g., political news, society news), the formats of news they consume (e.g., text, video), and the sources of the news (e.g., social media, news app) was uncovered.

2.1 Study participants

Since our study involved multiple stages, our participants varied based on which stage(s) they participated in. Our final stage participants, who completed the interview, had gone through all previous stages. Some participants completed the pre-diary survey but did not continue to complete the diary entries. Similarly, not all of the 51 participants who completed the diary studies participated in the follow-up interview. The sections below provide details on participants involved in different stages of our study.

2.1.1 Pre-diary survey participants (n = 63)

Table 2.1 shows the demographic information of participants who responded to our formal survey.

2.1.2 Diary study participants (n = 51)

Table 2.2 displays the demographic information of participants who participated in our diary study.

DOI: 10.4324/9781003053002-2

Table 2.1 Formal Survey Respondents' Demographic Information

Demographics		*n*	*%*
Gender	Male	16	25.4
	Female	47	74.6
Age group	Under 20	13	20.6
	20–24	36	57.1
	25–29	7	11.1
	30–40	6	9.5
	41–50	1	1.6
Ethnicity	American Indian	1	1.6
	Asian	19	30.2
	Black/African American	6	9.5
	Hispanic/Latino	9	14.3
	White/Caucasian	28	44.4
Class	Undergraduate	44	69.8
	Graduate	19	30.2
Major	Social sciences	25	36.8
	Sciences	19	27.9
	Arts & humanities	18	26.5
	Engineering	5	7.4
	Undeclared	1	1.5

Table 2.2 Diary Study Respondents' Demographic Information

Demographics		*n*	*%*
Gender	Female	36	70.6
	Male	15	29.4
Age group	Under 20	9	17.6
	20–24	31	60.8
	25–29	4	7.8
	30 or above	7	13.5
Ethnicity	American Indian	1	2.0
	Asian	15	29.4
	Black/African American	5	9.8
	Hispanic/Latino	7	13.5
	White/Caucasian	23	45.1
School	College	26	51.0
	University	24	47.1

(*Continued*)

Table 2.2 (Continued)

Demographics		*n*	*%*
	Other	1	2.0
Class	Freshman	5	9.8
	Sophomore	4	7.8
	Junior	5	9.8
	Senior	23	45.1
	Master's student	5	9.8
	Doctoral student	9	17.6
Type of student	American	42	82.4
	International	9	17.6
Major	Art & humanities	10	20.2
	Engineering	4	7.8
	Sciences	16	31.4
	Social sciences	20	39.2
	Undeclared	1	2.0

*2.1.3 Follow-up interview participants (*n *= 15)*

Table 2.3 displays the demographic information of interviewees who participated in our follow-up interviews.

2.2 Types of news

Various types of news are produced and consumed each day. Participants in our diary study, i.e., undergraduate and graduate students in the United States, consumed political news the most (35%). This could be due to the fact that this study was done a few months before and during the US 2016 presidential election. Participants also consumed a great deal of society news (18%), including news on social events or crime news; entertainment news (10%), including news on celebrities in the entertainment industry; sports news (9%); and science/technology news (9%). Other types of news that were consumed included public health news (4%) and commentary/opinion (4%). In total, there are a dozen types of news among the 522 news items participants submitted via the diary tool. Figure 2.1 shows the distribution of the types of news in the news items submitted by our participants.

Table 2.3 Interviewees' Demographic Information

Demographics		*n*	%
Gender	Male	2	13.3
	Female	13	86.7
Age group	Under 20	3	20.0
	20–24	9	60.0
	25–29	1	6.7
	30–40	1	6.7
	41–50	1	6.7
Ethnicity	Asian	4	26.7
	Black/African American	1	6.7
	Hispanic/Latino	1	6.7
	Multiple ethnicities	3	20.0
	White/Caucasian	6	40.0
School	California State University	1	6.7
	Emerson College	4	26.7
	Harvard University	1	6.7
	Rutgers University	1	6.7
	Simmons College	4	26.7
	University of Nebraska	1	6.7
	University of Texas, Austin	2	13.3
	University of Washington	1	6.7
Class	Freshman	1	6.7
	Sophomore	2	13.3
	Junior	2	13.3
	Senior	6	40.0
	Master's student	0	0.0
	Doctoral student	4	26.7
Type of student	American	13	86.7
	International	2	13.3
Nationality	Canada	1	6.7
	China	1	6.7
	Dual citizenship	2	13.3
	United States	11	73.3
Major	Astronomy	1	6.7
	Computer science	1	6.7
	Library & information science	1	6.7
	Marketing	1	6.7
	Multiple majors	5	33.3
	Sociology	2	13.3
	Undeclared	1	6.7
	Writing, literature, publishing	3	20.0

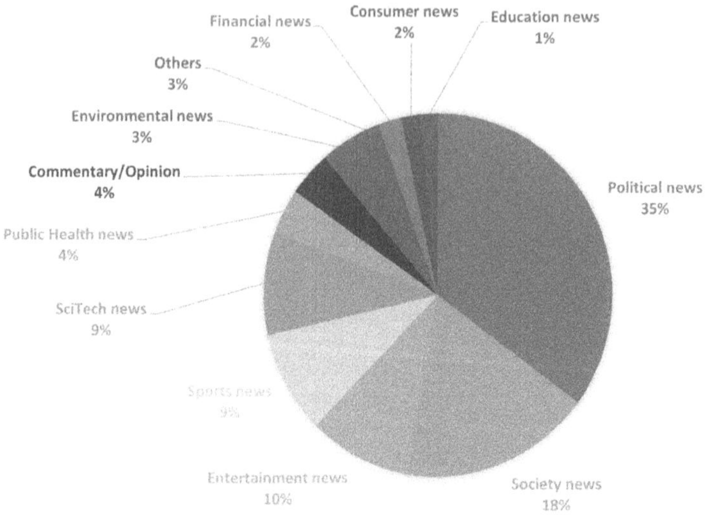

Figure 2.1 Types of News Consumption by Participants.

2.3 Sources of news

It is clear that university students consume many different types of news through their mobile phones, but where did they get the 522 news items submitted. The most common source of news that university students in the United States reported was social media (45.2%) such as Facebook, Twitter, or Instagram, which is noteworthy. As we can recall from the existing research, the types of news consumers included Net-Newsers (Pew Research Center, 2008) or digital news consumers (Schroder & Kobbernagel, 2010) who frequently consumed news from "net-based media." Both types of news consumers tend to receive their news from social media. Van Damme, Courtois, Verbrugge, and De Marez (2015) revealed that by consuming news through social media such as Facebook, people "stay updated" and "know what is going on … Traditional media did not lose their value, but mobile news has become important too" (p. 208, from a participant). For university students in our study, they were in a younger age group than the general public, so it is no surprise that the most common source of news was social media.

Our study also found that the second major source was the news app on their phone (41.0%). This is interesting when we compare our results with Van Damme et al.'s (2015) study of mobile news formats between news apps and news websites. The authors reported that people often consumed service-based news through the application. For instance, people used news apps to get "bite-sized updates," or to "check the weather forecast or public transport schedule in the morning" (p. 205). Note that with the advancement of technology, people are now used to relying on the news app to consume all kinds of news with more intensive texts instead of just weather or bus/train schedules.

For our study, the sources of news reported also included website (3.4%), email (3.1%), word of mouth (2.1%), TV (1.9%), and Google search (1.9%), but these were the sources of considerably lower numbers of news items when compared to social media or news apps, each of which represented over 40% of the news items reported in our study. Some of the traditional sources of news, such as newspaper (0.6%), magazine (0.6%), or radio (0.2%), were also sources included in our study, but they were each the source of less than 1% of the news items reported. This could be due to the fact that participants were using a mobile diary app and therefore had immediate access to their phone. Figure 2.2 displays the distribution of the sources of news in the news items submitted by our participants.

2.4 Formats of news

The format of news has also evolved greatly over the years. As indicated by Sheller (2015),

> As the means of production was transformed …, so too did the "interface" for receiving the newspaper also shift from newsprint on paper to website, and finally to tablet and mobile delivery of Web content. This was accompanied by the rise of enhanced visual media … more interactive features, and the development of near real-time blogs such as the Lede, with constantly updated stories.
>
> (p. 16)

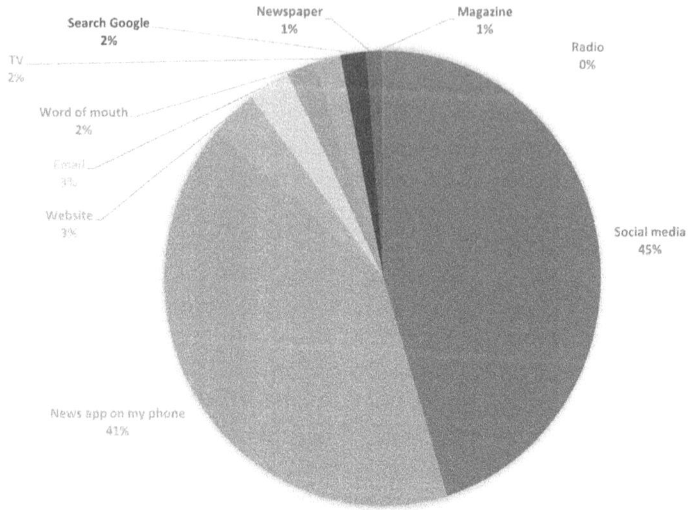

Figure 2.2 Sources of News Consumed by Participants.

When people read news from print newspapers, the news is formatted either as text or text and image (photo). When news is consumed through radio, the format is audio, and when it's on TV, the format is video. Now, university students are actively consuming news through their mobile phones, and the new items are no longer limited to just one or two formats. Our data showed that the most common format of mobile news consumed by university students was still text (48.5%), followed by text and image (photo) (28.7%). However, there were several other formats, such as a combination of text, video, and image (photo) (7.9%), text and video (7.7%), and video (4.2%). There were also news items with only image (photo) (0.8%); a combination of text, audio, video, and image (photo) (0.8%); text, audio, and image (photo) (0.6%); and text, video, and audio (0.6%). Although there were very few cases, there were also audio (0.2%) only and video and image (photo) (0.2%). This showed that while traditional formats are still used, several new formats were consumed through mobile phones in multimedia presentations. The distribution of the formats of news

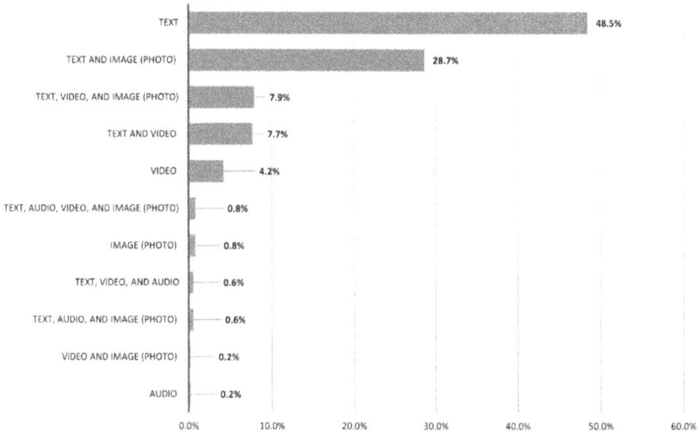

Figure 2.3 Formats of News Consumed by Participants.

in the news items submitted by our participants is presented in Figure 2.3.

2.5 Demographic differences

Demographic differences mean that people with various demographic attributes might consume news differently through their smartphones. There were some differences in the types, sources, and formats of news that the study participants consumed based on their demographic characteristics.

2.5.1 Demographics and the types of news

Existing research indicated that demographic attributes have an impact on the types of news people consumed (e.g., Taneja, Webster, Malthouse, & Ksiazek, 2012; Van Damme et al., 2015). In our study, as shown in Table 2.4, the top three types of news consumed by each age group were all from four types of news: Political news, society news, sports news, and entertainment news. Among those, political news was the type of news that was consumed the most by participants in all age groups. However,

Table 2.4 Top Three Types of News Consumed by Participants in Different Age Groups

Age Group	*Top Three Types of News*
Under 20	Political news (41.5%), sports news (13.2%), society news (11.3%)
20–24	Political news (33.0%), society news (19.6%), entertainment news (11.9%)
25–29	Political news (36.0%), entertainment news (16.0%), society news (12.0%)
30 or above	Political news (34.4%), society news (20.3%), sports news (10.9%)

entertainment news was one of the top three types of news consumed by only younger participants (people in their 20s), and sports news was one of the top three types of news consumed by people who are both young (under 20) and middle aged (above 30). The statistical analysis showed that these differences are statistically significant.

In our study, academic specializations or disciplines played a role in the types of news consumed. Students in varying specializations consumed news of different kinds differently, as displayed in Table 2.5. Political news was consumed the most by participants in all majors. However, only 26.7% of the news consumed by arts & humanities students was political news, which was much lower than students in other majors (33.6–58.3%). In addition, arts & humanities students consumed science/technology news more than students in other majors, while science/technology news was not included in the top three types of news among sciences, social sciences, and engineering students. Interestingly, although with slight differences in the percentage, the top three types of news were the same, and in the same order, for sciences students and engineering students. Social sciences students showed similar patterns, except that sports news was not among their top three types of news while entertainment news was. Students with undeclared majors consumed political news more than students in other majors, and then consumed five different types of news, including environmental news and financial news, which didn't appear in the top three types of news consumed by students in other majors.

Table 2.5 Top Three Types of News Consumed by Participants in Different Majors

Major	*Top Three Types of News*
Sciences	Political news (41.2%), society news (17.6%), sports news (12.5%)
Social sciences	Political news (33.6%), society news (21.2%), entertainment news (10.6%)
Engineering	Political news (40.5%), society news (18.9%), sports news (13.5%)
Arts & humanities	Political news (26.7%), science/technology news (21.7%), entertainment news (11.7%), society news (11.7%)
Undeclared	Political news (58.3%), environmental news (8.3%), financial news (8.3%), science/technology news (8.3%), society news (8.3%), sports news (8.3%)

Table 2.6 Top Three Types of News Consumed by Undergraduate and Graduate Participants

Class	*Top Three Types of News*
Undergraduate	Political news (35.1%), society news (15.6%), entertainment news (10.6%)
Graduate	Political news (34.7%), society news (24.6%), commentary and opinion (8.5%), sports news (8.5%)

For this study, we grouped students in all classes into two categories: Undergraduate and graduate. Both undergraduate and graduate students consumed political news the most; over one-third of the news they consumed was political news. The second top news type was society news for both undergraduate and graduate students, but consumption was higher among graduate students than among undergraduates. Interestingly, entertainment news appeared as one of the top three types of news only for undergraduate students. In a similar vein, commentary, and opinion as well as sports news were listed among the top three news types only for graduate students. The results are presented in Table 2.6.

Our analyses showed that there were no statistically significant differences between types of news and participants' gender, ethnicity, and student type (i.e., international, American).

2.5.2 Demographic differences in the sources of news

While previous research has examined the types of media that people relied on as their sources of news (e.g., Schroder & Kobbernagel, 2010; Van Damme et al., 2015), we were not only interested in learning what sources of news were most popular among our participants, but also in learning whether there were differences among various demographic groups in their sources of news. Tables 2.7–2.10 show those demographic groups that had significant differences in their sources of news.

Specifically, in terms of sources of news used by people of different age groups, the news app on my phone was selected as

Table 2.7 Top Three Sources of News Consumed by Participants in Different Age Groups

Age Group	*Top Three Sources of News*
Under 20	News app on my phone (59.4%), website (25.5%), search Google (6.6%)
20–24	News app on my phone (45.3%), website (44.6%), search Google (3.1%)
25–29	News app on my phone (36.0%), website (24.0%), email (20.0%)
30 or above	Website (54.7%), news app on my phone (25.0%), magazine (17.2%)

Table 2.8 Top Three Sources of News Consumed by Undergraduate and Graduate Participants

Class	*Top Three Sources of News*
Undergraduate	Social media (46.8%), news app on my phone (40.1%), website (4.5%)
Graduate	News app on my phone (44.1%), social media (39.8%), email (10.2%)

Table 2.9 Top Three Sources of News Consumed by Participants in Different Ethnicities

Ethnicity	*Top Three Sources of News*
American Indian	Social media (50.0%), website (25.0%), newspaper (16.7%)
Asian	Social media (50.7%), news app on my phone (34.7%), website (6.3%)
Black/African American	News app on my phone (79.4%), social media (11.8%), TV (5.9%)
Hispanic/Latino	News app on my phone (49.4%), social media (37.6%), TV (4.7%)
White/Caucasian	Social media (49.0%), news app on my phone (38.1%), email (4.5%)

Table 2.10 Top Three Sources of News Consumed by Participants in Different Majors

Major	*Top Three Sources of News*
Sciences	News app on my phone (48.5%), social media (40.4%), website (5.9%)
Social sciences	Social media (43.3%), news app on my phone (41.0%), email (5.5%)
Engineering	Social media (51.4%), news app on my phone (43.2%), radio (2.7%), TV (2.7%)
Arts & humanities	Social media (47.5%), news app on my phone (35.8%), search Google (5.8%)
Undeclared	Social media (91.7%), word of mouth (8.3%)

one of the top three sources across all age groups. Among age groups under 30, the news app on my phone is the most popular source, while it was the second most popular source for people ages above 30. The website is another popular source, ranked as the second most popular source for participants aged under 30 and the most popular source for participants older than 30 years of age. Another top three source for age groups under 25 years was search Google, while for the 25–29 age group, email was the third most popular source. Interestingly, for participants older than 29 years of age, magazines were the third most popular source.

We also found that undergraduate students' preference for sources of news differed significantly from those of graduate students. While social media was the top choice for undergraduates, it was the second choice for graduate students. News app was the number one choice for graduate students, and it was number two for undergraduate students. Since undergraduate students are a younger and mostly digital native generation, the fact that social media is their number one choice for news is not strange; however, relying heavily on news fed through social media, the undergraduate students should be better equipped with online reason and digital literacy skills in order to separate accurate news reporting from fake news.

In terms of preferences for sources of news, three ethnic groups (American Indian, Asian, and White/Caucasian) had social media as their top choice, whereas Black/African American and Hispanic/Latino participants had the news app as their top choice. What is also interesting is that for Black/African American and Hispanic/Latino participants, even though they share the same preference for the news app as other ethnic groups, their third most common choice was TV, which is different from American Indian, Asian, and White/Caucasian participants. American Indian participants also preferred newspapers as a news source, while White/Caucasian participants used emails as their top source. For American Indian and Asian participants, news websites were also among the top three preferred sources.

All participants except students with science majors preferred social media as their source of news. In particular, participants who didn't declare their major used social media as their main source of news (91.7%). In the case of students with sciences majors, their preferred source of news was "news app on my phone," which was the second most popular source of news for students with social sciences, engineering, and arts & humanities majors. Interestingly, website was one of the top three sources of news only for sciences majors, email was one of the top three sources of news only for social sciences majors, radio and TV appeared in the top three sources of news only for engineering students, search Google was one of the top sources only for arts & humanities students, and word of mouth was one of the top sources only for the participants who had not yet declared their majors.

Note that there were no statistically significant differences between sources of news and participants' gender and student type (i.e., international, American).

2.5.3 Demographic differences in the formats of news

We analyzed whether there are demographic differences in the formats of news that participants consumed and found differences based on their age groups. A pure text format was used the most by all age groups except those who were between 25 and 29. For this age group, text and image/photo was the most common format, and text was the second most common. For other age groups, the text and image/photo format was the second most common format of news consumed by participants. Another popular format was text and video, which appeared in all age groups' top three formats of news other than those who were between 20 and 29. The top three formats of news consumed by different age groups are presented in Table 2.11.

We also analyzed whether there are differences in news formats among students in different majors. Text was still the most common news format for students with different majors, except for students who had not yet declared their majors. In particular, engineering students heavily consumed news in the pure text format (73.0%). Another interesting news consumption behavior of the engineering students was consuming news in an audio format. This format

Table 2.11 Top Three Formats of News Consumed by Participants in Different Age Groups

Age Group	*Top Three Formats of News*
Under 20	Text (54.7%), text and image/photo (25.5%), text and video (9.4%)
20–24	Text (51.1%), text and image/photo (28.1%), text and video (6.7%)
25–29	Text and image/photo (36.0%), text, video, and image/photo (28.0%), video (8.0%), image/photo (8.0%), text, audio, video, and image/photo (8.0%)
30 or above	Text (42.2%), text and image/photo (34.4%), text and video (10.9%), text, video, and image/photo (10.9%)

Table 2.12 Top Three Formats of News Consumed by Participants in Different Majors

Major	*Top Three Formats of News*
Sciences	Text (58.8%), video (18.4%), text and image/photo (10.3%)
Social sciences	Text (41.9%), video (35.9%), text, audio, and image/photo (11.1%)
Engineering	Text (73.0%), audio (10.8%), text and image/photo (10.8%)
Arts & humanities	Text (45.8%), video (34.2%), text and image/photo (5.8%)
Undeclared	Text, audio, and image/photo (50.0%), video (41.7%), text and image/photo (8.3%)

didn't appear in any of the students in different majors' top three news formats, but it was the second most frequently consumed news type for the engineering students. Video was the second most used format in all majors other than engineering students. The top three formats of news used by participants in different majors are displayed in Table 2.12.

In terms of ethnicity, we also found some differences. Text was again the most used form among all ethnicities except Hispanic/Latino. In the case of the Hispanic/Latino participants, text and image/photo was the most consumed news format. The text format was especially popular among American Indian and Black/African American participants (91.7% and 91.2%, respectively). Text and image/photo was the most consumed news format by Hispanic/Latino participants and the second most consumed news format by all the other participants, which indicated that it's one of the main formats of news consumed by participants. Table 2.13 presents the top three formats of news used by participants in different ethnicities.

Our analyses showed that there were no statistically significant differences between news format and participants' gender, student class (i.e., graduate, undergraduate), and student type (i.e., international, American).

Table 2.13 Top Three Formats of News Consumed by Participants in Different Ethnicities

Ethnicity	*Top Three Formats of News*
American Indian	Text (91.7%), text and image/photo (8.3%)
Asian	Text (52.1%), text and image/photo (21.5%), text and video (13.2%)
Black/African American	Text (91.2%), text and image/photo (5.9%), video (2.9%)
Hispanic/Latino	Text and image/photo (36.5%), text (34.1%), text and video (9.4%), text, video, and image/photo (9.4%)
White/Caucasian	Text (43.3%), text and image/photo (34.4%), text, video, and image/photo (11.7%)

2.6 Summary

In this chapter, we describe the news consumed by our study participants through their mobile phones. We report the types of news (e.g., political news, society news, environmental news), the format of news (e.g., images, text, videos), and the source of news (e.g., social media, news app, newspaper) our participants consumed during the study period. We also report statistically significant demographic differences. These include differences in gender, age groups, ethnicity, students' academic status and academic interests, and how they affect the types, formats, and sources of news they consume.

References

Pew Research Center. (2008). *Key news audiences now blend online and traditional sources*. Retrieved from www.pewresearch.org/politics/2008/08/17/key-news-audiences-now-blend-onlineand-traditional-sources/

Schroder, K. C., & Kobbernagel, C. (2010). Towards a typology of cross-media news consumption: A qualitative quantitative synthesis. *Northern Lights: Film and Media Studies Yearbook, 8*(1), 115–137. https://doi.org/10.1386/nl.8.115_1

Sheller, M. (2015). News now. *Journalism Studies, 16*(1), 12–26. https://doi.org/10.1080/1461670X.2014.890324

Taneja, H., Webster, J. G., Malthouse, E. C., & Ksiazek, T. B. (2012). Media consumption across platforms: Identifying user-defined repertoires. *New Media & Society, 14*(6), 951–968. https://doi.org/10.1177/1461444811436146

Van Damme, K., Courtois, C., Verbrugge, K., & De Marez, L. (2015). What's APPening to news? A mixed-method audience-centred study on mobile news consumption. *Mobile Media & Communication, 3*(2), 196–213. https://doi.org/10.1177/2050157914557691

3 Mobile News Consumption Cycle and Activities

When people consume news through their mobile devices, their behavioral patterns and activities might be distinctly different from how they consume news through other media, such as TV or newspapers. On the other hand, it should be noted that in daily life, the consumption of news through mobile devices is frequently intertwined with consuming news using other media. In this chapter, based on what we learned from our research studies, we outline the consumption cycle and how various activities, including receiving, reading, finding, sharing, and storing news, are anchored on the mobile tools users have, the functionality and features of the mobile news apps, and the mobile users' characteristics and preferences.

3.1 Receiving/noticing news

In consuming news from their mobile devices, people may have a distinct path of receiving and thereby noticing news items. In our studies, we have both quantitative data from a diary study and qualitative data from the following interviews. Demographic differences were examined with regard to differences among the reasons that participants noticed news items or the parts of news items that drew their attention to the news story. Most of our data reveal a pattern in news noticing behavior.

DOI: 10.4324/9781003053002-3

Table 3.1 Reasons for Participants to Notice or Receive News from Mobile Devices

Reasons (not mutually exclusive)	#	%
Interesting headline or story	362	69.3
Main/trending/popular story (breaking news)	43	8.2
Surprising/weird story	23	4.4
Related to (or shared by) my friends/family	23	4.4
N/A (no explanation, don't know)	1	0.2

3.1.1 Reasons for receiving/noticing news items

For our diary study, participants were asked to note down their "primary reasons for noticing the news item" for each news story that they submitted to the diary system. There were five primary reasons for participants noticing a news item: The most common reason was an interesting headline or story (*n* = 362, 69%). Participants' attention was also drawn to a news story because they received a notification via news feed, alert, or other form of mobile notification (*n* = 70, 13.4%). Trending or breaking news for the day also caught people's attention (*n* = 43, 8.4%). While surprising/weird news attracted participants' attention (*n* = 23, 4.4%), stories related to or shared by their family or friends received equal amounts of attention (*n* = 23, 4.4%). Table 3.1 lists the reasons that participants noticed news stories.

3.1.1.1 Gender

Significant gender differences were found in terms of what drew participants' attention to a news story. For instance, more female participants than male participants were attracted to a news story due to its interesting headline (female 70.9% and male 65.8%), its status as trending/breaking news (female 8.9% and male 6.8%), or it having been shared by or related to their friends/families (female 5.5% and male 1.9%). Interestingly, more male participants (5.0%) reported they were drawn to surprising or weird stories than female participants (4.2%).

Table 3.2 Top 3 Reasons for Participants of Various Age Groups to Notice or Receive News from Mobile Devices

Age Groups	*Top 1*	*Top 2*	*Top 3*
Under 20	Interesting headline or story	Provided (news feed, alert, notification, newsletter, front page)	Main/trending/popular story (breaking news)
20–24	Interesting headline or story	Provided (news feed, alert, notification, newsletter, front page)	Main/trending/popular story (breaking news)
25–29	Interesting headline or story	Related to (or shared by) my friends/ family	Main/trending/popular story (breaking news)
30 or above	Interesting headline or story	Provided (news feed, alert, notification, newsletter, front page)	Main/trending/popular story (breaking news)

3.1.1.2 Age group

Significant differences were also found among various age groups with regard to what drew them to the news stories. For instance, significantly higher proportions of the news stories were noticed because they were related to or shared by friends and family for people in the age group of 25–29 years of age (20.0%) than people under 20 (3.8%), people ages 20–24 (3.7%), or people ages 30 or above (3.1%). Overall, however, there are similarities among the top reasons that attracted participants of various age groups. Table 3.2 shows the top three reasons for the four age groups.

3.1.1.2 Classes

In terms of classes, significant differences were found among various class levels with regard to what drew them to the news stories. While "Interesting headline or story" was the number 1 reason for students of all academic levels, the top 2 or 3 reasons varied from "Provided (news feed, alert, notification, newsletter, front page)" to "Main /trending /popular story (breaking news)," "Related to (or shared by) my friends /family," and "Surprising weird story." Table 3.3 displays the top three reasons for participants of various classes.

Table 3.3 Top 3 Reasons for Participants of Various Classes to Notice or Receive News from Mobile Devices

Classes	*Top 1*	*Top 2*	*Top 3*
Freshman	Interesting headline or story	Provided (news feed, alert, notification, newsletter, front page)	Main/trending/popular story (breaking news)
Sophomore	Interesting headline or story	Surprising weird story	• Main/trending/ popular story (breaking news) • Related to (or shared by) my friends/family • Provided (news feed, alert, notification, newsletter, front page)
Junior	Interesting headline or story	Related to (or shared by) my friends/family	• Main/trending/ popular story (breaking news) • Provided (news feed, alert, notification, newsletter, front page)
Senior	Interesting headline or story	Main/trending/ popular story (breaking news)	Surprising weird story
Master's student	Interesting headline or story	Provided (news feed, alert, notification, newsletter, front page)	Main/trending/popular story (breaking news)
Doctoral student	Interesting headline or story	Main/trending/ popular story (breaking news)	Related to (or shared by) my friends/family

3.1.1.3 Majors or academic specializations

With regard to differences among students of various majors, significant differences were found among them with regard to what drew them to the news stories. While "Interesting headline or story" was the number 1 reason for students of all majors or specializations, the number 2 reason varied between "Provided (news feed, alert, notification, newsletter, front page)" and "Main/trending/popular story (breaking news)." And number 3 reasons varied from "Related to (or shared by) my friends/family" to "Provided (news feed, alert, notification, newsletter, front page)," "Main/trending/popular story (breaking news)," and "Surprising weird story." Table 3.4 presents the top three reasons for participants of various majors.

Table 3.4 Top 3 Reasons for Participants of Various Majors to Notice or Receive News from Mobile Devices

Major	*Top 1*	*Top 2*	*Top 3*
Arts & humanities	Interesting headline or story	Provided (news feed, alert, notification, newsletter, front page)	Main/trending/popular story (breaking news)
Sciences	Interesting headline or story	Main/trending/popular story (breaking news)	• Surprising weird story • Provided (news feed, alert, notification, newsletter, front page)
Social sciences	Interesting headline or story	Provided (news feed, alert, notification, newsletter, front page)	Related to (or shared by) my friends/family
Engineering	Interesting headline or story	Main/trending/popular story (breaking news)	Provided (news feed, alert, notification, newsletter, front page)
Undeclared	Interesting headline or story	Provided (news feed, alert, notification, newsletter, front page)	Related to (or shared by) my friends/family

3.1.1.4 Additional reasons for noticing news

From our follow-up interviews, participants shared several additional reasons for receiving news using their mobile devices. Several participants actually received their news by accident. Participants used the term "stumbled upon it" to describe how they encountered news. As P26 shared in their story of receiving/noticing a news story –

> I actually – I was listening, I was changing the radio, and I was seeking, with the seek button and I started to listen to this, uh, I think it was BBC, so they started talking about it and I listened to it for a while.

Another reason for noticing or receiving news was being bored and wanting to find something on the news, as described by P13 as their regular habit: "When I am bored or when I want to find something on the news, I'll use that news app."

In terms of describing the sources where they received news, five interviewees indicated that they received the news from their mobile news app or aggregators. As pointed out by P21, "the main one I use is called SmartNews. Um, it's a news aggregator and I think that was the only one that I was using when I used the app." Participants also mentioned social media or computers/websites as a common source of receiving their news story. P50 relied on two popular social media platforms for news: "I get a lot of my news from social media … mostly Facebook and Twitter. Mostly Twitter, because usually people tweet more reliable sources than on Facebook." Participants also used computers to follow up to get more detailed information about a new story. As P1 described,

> I use computer if I'm interested in the story, like the Bangladesh attack. Later on I used computer, laptop to Google the things because with a bigger screen and, it's just my personal opinion, I think through computer access Google can provide more information than even a mobile set, especially some links provided by Google, can only show regularly or normally on a computer screen, but not a mobile screen.

Other sources included email alerts, word of mouth, or radio. P6 got their news frequently from email:

> I found the best way for me to at least get some news during the day was just to have to sign up for papers and to just have them email me directly. And so over time I've just kind of -- New York Times.

P50 obtained really funny and outrageous news from their friends, and "whenever I'm with, like, with my roommate or my boyfriend, we usually talk about, some, either, funny or, really interesting, news stuff."

The interviewees also commented on the sources which they did not rely on to receive their news. These included "Not from TV," "Not from radio," "Not from newspaper," or "Not from computer." While P1 indicated that "I didn't use radio or TV," P10 usually didn't use any other media including newspaper, TV, or their computer to get more information about the story.

3.1.2 Parts of news stories drawing people's attention

When it comes to which parts of the news stories drew people's attention when first receiving the news, our study results show that participants mainly noticed the news based on its content ($n = 378$, 72.4%). Much less frequently, the title or headline of the news ($n = 47$, 9%) or images ($n = 9$, 1.7%) also drew some attention. Figure 3.1 displays the frequency of the reasons for noticing the news stories.

There are also demographic differences among different groups of people in terms of which part of the news stories drew their attention. The following sections will report on these differences.

3.1.2.1 Gender

Significant gender differences were found in terms of what part of the news stories drew participants' attention. More female participants than male participants were attracted to a news story due to its content (female 74.5% and male 67.7%), its title or headlines (female 10.2% and male 6.2%), or its image/photos/

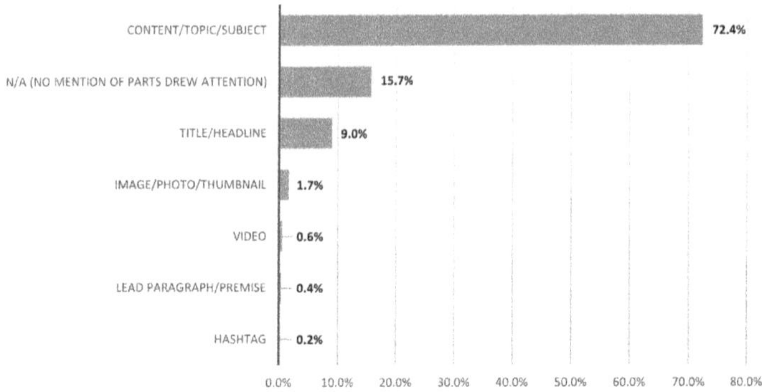

Figure 3.1 Parts of the News Used by Participants in Noticing the News Items.

graphic/thumbnails (female 1.9% and male 1.2%). Interestingly, more male participants (0.6%) reported they were drawn to Lead Paragraph/Premise than female participants (0.3%). Furthermore, while a few female participants were drawn to a story because of its video (0.8%) or its hashtag (0.3%), none of the male participants indicated that they were drawn to the stories because of the video or hashtag.

Despite the proportional differences, the top parts that drew both female and male participants were in the same order: Content /topic/ subject, Title/headline, then Image/graphic/photo or thumbnail.

3.1.2.2 Classes

Significant differences were also found among various classes with regard to which part of the news stories they noticed when they first received the news. For instance, significantly higher proportions of the news stories were noticed because of their titles or headlines for participants in the master's program (18.6%) and juniors (18.3%) than people in the PhD programs (9.3%), freshmen (6.7%), seniors (6.3%), and sophomores (4.3%). Overall, however, there are similarities among the top sections of the news items that attracted participants of various class levels. Table 3.5 shows the top three sections/parts for the six classes. As shown in Table 3.5, while

Table 3.5 Top 3 Sections of the News Stories that Drew Participants of Various Class Levels' Attention

Classes	*Top 1*	*Top 2*	*Top 3*
Freshman	Content/topic/ subject	Title/headline	None
Sophomore	Content/topic/ subject	Title/headline	Video
Junior	Content/topic/ subject	Title/headline	Image/graphic/photo/ thumbnail
Senior	Content/topic/ subject	Title/headline	Image/graphic/photo/ thumbnail
Master's student	Content/topic/ subject	Title/headline	Video Lead Paragraph or Premise hashtag
Doctoral student	Content/topic/ subject	Title/headline	Image/graphic/photo/ thumbnail

"Content/topic/subject" and "Title/headline" were the number one and number two parts that drew all class groups' attention, for number three, "Image/graphic/photo/thumbnail" was the section that drew junior, senior, or doctoral students' attention, and "video" was the number three section that attracted sophomore or master's students' attention. The master's students were also drawn by the lead paragraph or hashtags. Table 3.5 presents the top three sections of the news stories that drew the attention of the participants of various class levels.

3.1.2.3 Majors

With regard to students of various majors, significant differences were found among them with regard to which sections of the news stories drew their attention when first noticing or receiving the news story. For instance, a higher proportion of news stories were noticed because of their "Title/headlines" by students majoring in the social sciences (12.4%) than those majoring in the sciences (11.8%) or arts & humanities (3.3%). Both students majoring in engineering and students who had not yet declared a major did not report noticing a news story because of its "Title/headline."

In terms of the top three sections that drew people's attention, all major groups listed "Content/topic/subject" as their number

Table 3.6 Top 3 Sections that Participant of Various Majors Noticed When Receiving News from Mobile Devices

Major	*Top 1*	*Top 2*	*Top 3*
Arts & humanities	Content/topic/subject	• Title/headline • Image/graphic/photo/thumbnail	Video
Sciences	Content/topic/subject	Title/headline	Image/graphic/photo/thumbnail
Social sciences	Content/topic/subject	Title/Headline	Image/graphic/photo/thumbnail
Engineering	Content/topic/subject	• Video • Hashtag	None
Undeclared	Content/topic/subject	None	None

1 section. The number 2 section varied from "Title/Headline" to "Image/graphic/photo/thumbnail," "Video," and "Hashtag." And the number 3 section varied between "Video" and "Image/graphic/photo/thumbnail." Table 3.6 lists the top three sections of the news stories that drew people's attention when they noticed and received the news stories via their mobile devices.

3.2 Reading news

After receiving and noticing news, people start reading the news on their mobile devices. In terms of reading behaviors, people varied from reading the news story fully to scanning headlines or lead paragraphs. Demographic differences were found not only in news consumption activities but also in reading methods. Additional insights about reading behaviors, the reasons for reading or not reading a news story, as well as the reading methods were obtained from the qualitative follow-up interviews.

3.2.1 News reading behavior

In this section, we discuss the demographic differences in people's news-reading behavior. We discovered that there were significant differences among various gender, ethnicity, school type, and major groups. The specific differences are outlined next.

3.2.1.1 Demographic differences

3.2.1.1.1 GENDER

There were statistically significant differences in reading/watching news between participants of different genders. A significantly higher proportion of news stories were read and watched by female participants than by male participants.

3.2.1.1.2 ETHNICITY

There were statistically significant differences in reading/watching mobile news behavior among participants of different ethnicities. A significantly higher proportion of news stories were read or watched by Hispanic/Latino participants, Black/African American participants, and American Indian participants than by White/Caucasian participants and Asian participants.

3.2.1.1.3 SCHOOL TYPE

Statistically significant differences were found among school type and reading/watching mobile news. A significantly higher proportion of news stories were read and watched by participants from institutions other than universities or colleges than by participants from colleges or participants from universities.

3.2.1.1.4 MAJOR

There were statistically significant differences in reading/watching mobile behavior among participants in different majors. A significantly higher proportion of news stories were read and watched by arts & humanities students and students with undeclared majors than by social science students, science students, or engineering students.

3.2.2 Methods of reading

3.2.2.1 Overall methods of reading

From our diary study, we found that among the 481 news items read by the participants, 310 of them (64.4%) were read by reading

Table 3.7 Participants' Reading Behavior

Reading Behavior	#	%
Read the full news story closely	310	64.4
Skim the main parts of the news story	125	26.0
Scan the headlines/lead paragraphs	45	9.4
Other	1	0.2
Total	481	100.0

the full news story closely, and 125 news items (26.0%) were read by skimming the main parts of the news story. Interestingly, 45 news items (9.4%) were read by scanning the headlines or lead paragraphs. One item (0.2%) was shared by another method. With more than half of the news stories read in full, it is interesting how university students digest the majority of mobile news in its entirety to get the full story. Table 3.7 shows the various reading extents of participants.

3.2.2.2 Demographic differences in reading methods

In addition to the general news reading behavior, we also found significant differences among age groups, ethnicity groups, classes, and majors in how they read the news.

3.2.2.2.1 AGE GROUP

In terms of specific reading methods, the age group in which the highest proportion of participants "read the full news story closely" was those who were 25–29 years old. The age group that had the highest proportion of participants who "skimmed the main parts of the news story" was people 20–24 years old. The highest proportion of participants who "scanned the headlines/lead paragraphs" was people under 20 years old. Note that despite all the proportional differences, "read the full news story closely" was the most common method for all age groups, and "skimmed the main parts of the news story" was the second most common method across all age groups. For "scanned the headlines/lead paragraphs," no participant in the age group of 25–29 years used this method, whereas the remaining three groups used it as their third most common method of reading.

3.2.2.2.2 ETHNICITY

Interestingly, the ethnic group with the highest proportion of participants who "read the full news story closely" was Black/African American. The ethnic group in which the highest proportion of participants "skimmed the main parts of the news story" was Asian. The ethnic group in which the highest proportion of participants "scanned the headlines/lead paragraphs" was American Indian. Note that despite all the proportional differences, with one exception, "read the full news story closely" was the most common method for all ethnic groups, "skimmed the main parts of the news story" was the second most common method across all ethnic groups, and "scanned the headlines/lead paragraphs" was the third most common reading method for all groups. The one exception was among the American Indian participants; in this group, there were equal numbers of news stories read using each of the three methods.

3.2.2.2.3 CLASS

For using specific reading methods, the class in which the highest proportion of participants "read the full news story closely" was doctoral students. The class that had the highest proportion of participants who "skimmed the main parts of the news story" was master's students. Meanwhile, the class with the highest proportion of participants who "scanned the headlines/lead paragraphs" was sophomores. Similarly to the previously discussed demographic groups, despite all the proportional differences, "read the full news story closely" was the most common method for all class groups, "skimmed the main parts of the news story" was the second most common method across all groups, and "scanned the headlines/lead paragraphs" was the third most common reading method for all groups. For the "freshman" group, there were equal numbers of news stories read through "skimmed the main parts of the news story" and "scanned the headlines/lead paragraphs."

Table 3.8 Top 3 Methods of Reading by Majors

Major	*Top 1*	*Top 2*	*Top 3*
Arts & humanities	Read the full news story closely	Skimmed the main parts of the news story	Scanned the headlines/lead paragraphs
Sciences	Read the full news story closely	Skimmed the main parts of the news story	Scanned the headlines/lead paragraphs
Social sciences	Read the full news story closely	Skimmed the main parts of the news story	Scanned the headlines/lead paragraphs
Engineering	Skimmed the main parts of the news story	Read the full news story closely	Scanned the headlines/lead paragraphs
Undeclared	scanned the headlines/lead paragraphs	read the full news story closely	None

3.2.2.2.4 MAJOR

In terms of specific reading methods, the highest proportion of participants who "read the full news story closely" was majoring in social sciences. The highest proportion of participants who "skimmed the main parts of the news story" was majoring in engineering. The highest proportion of participants who "scanned the headlines/lead paragraphs" was people with undeclared majors. Interestingly, "read the full news story closely" was the most common reading method for students majoring in arts & humanities, social sciences, and sciences, while "skimmed the main parts of the news story" was the number one reading method for students majoring in engineering, and "scanned the headlines/lead paragraphs" was the most common method of reading for students with undeclared majors. Table 3.8 lists the common methods of reading for all major groups.

3.2.3 Additional insights about reading behavior and methods

Our follow-up interviews provided further insights into participants' reading behavior, reasons for reading or not reading news on their mobile devices, various reading methods, and the reasons for using certain reading techniques.

3.2.3.1 Reading behavior

Participants in our follow-up interviews described to us their reading behavior. Multiple participants commented on the convenience of reading news on their phones. For instance, one participant (P13) commented, "using a phone is more convenient than using a laptop just because a phone is so small, I can read it when I'm walking to class." Another participant (P21) indicated that "I normally read news on my phone to pass time when I'm out and about." A third participant (P40) summarized it well: "I am probably going to be more inclined to read news on my phone, because it's more convenient. It kind of, like with the NYT it comes to me rather than me having to actually search for something." P40 further stated that they read news when commuting: "I commute to school and work, so I'll use my phone a lot during the commute to pass the time. I typically use my computer in the evenings on the weekdays, when I've gotten home."

For several participants, mobile devices were the starting point for them to read about a news item. If they wished to follow up a particular news story, they would use other online resources. As commented by P01, "We follow up just like read more materials like books or online resources." However, depending on the content of the story or the interest in the story, participants may choose not to follow up. For instance, P10 mentioned that they did not want to find anything extra for "that whole fiasco with the Trump Tower … there was more information coming in and coming in and I wasn't necessarily looking for it but I kept finding it."

There were several interesting reading behaviors reported from our conversations with the participants. For example, participants commented on how they got to read a series of news in the same day. As pointed out by P11, "A lot of the articles that I read, they're all in the same day. So if I read one article, then that will inform what I read for my next article sometimes, depending on what the content is." For complicated stories or news items that had video components, participants would turn to computers for reading news. P50 indicated that they were not prone to watching videos on their phone as opposed to on their computer. "But on the computer, I can keep the video open while I'm reading. So that can help me understand sometimes." P18 also commented on using a computer to "read longer messa-uh, sorry, longer news articles … and also ones with more complex kind of content."

3.2.3.2 Reasons for reading or not reading mobile news

In the follow-up interviews, participants discussed the reasons for deciding to read or not to read a news story. Table 3.9 provides a list of common reasons for reading or not reading news on their mobile phones, such as interestingness, personal interest, headline attractiveness, or being valuable, as well as selected comments from the participants.

Other reasons that were uniquely attributed to why participants read a news story were: To learn more about the news, to be informed; to follow up with similar news; to get context for a news story; to know what others think about the news; or to read a news story recommended by their friends. For instance, P50 commented, "Usually if it's saying, informing me of things that I haven't heard of before, I'll try to take more time to read it." P37 also specified, "I mostly just look or read news that are informative." P43 would follow up with similar news stories, "If I read something and then I see another headline that's sort of similar to it, then I'm more likely to click on it, just because I just read something on it and what is this one about now."

3.2.3.3 Reading methods

With various reading methods such as "Read the full news story closely," "Skim the main parts of the news story," or "Scan the headlines/lead paragraphs," we discussed with the participants in the follow-up interviews what their reading habits were and how exactly they read their mobile news. Participants' comments also revealed another method, which is scrolling through the article first before reading it. Table 3.10 lists some examples of how participants described their specific reading methods and the reasons they chose to use certain methods.

3.3 Finding news

In addition to receiving news from news app feeds or recommendations from friends, family, or acquaintances, people also actively search and find information on their own. While some of them used search engines, others searched social media for news. Demographic differences were found in news finding

Table 3.9 Common Reasons for Reading or Not Reading News

Common Themes for Reasons	*Reasons for Reading*	*Reasons for Not Reading*	*Example Comments*
Interestingness	Interesting	Not interesting	• I think I have a focus more on titles, um, because you guys asked why, or the-what did you, like-something about the title or something about what caught me to the article and usually it was the title...for me. (P26)
Personal interest	Personal interest	Not interested	• I'm also an African-American woman and the current politi-um, political and social state that we're in, so, um, many reasons for clicking on the news stories that I click on. Um, academic, professional, and personal. (P21) • Unless it's about a topic that really interests me and I think is really important, and then I'll read all of it. (P43)
Headline attractiveness	Headline of big breaking news	Headline too long or too specific	• My first concern is whether it is like the big news of breaking news of the day. (P1) • I guess if the topic is something I'm not really interested, or if the headline seems a little bit too long and too specific, I would be like, I kind of got the gist of it already, so I just want to move on or look at something else. (P37)
Valuable	Important	Not valuable	• Unless it's about a topic that really really interests me and I think is really important, and then I'll read all of it. (P43). • I use news app in my iphone so if I am not interested in it or I think it is invaluable I won't read it. (P1)
	Affects a lot of people		• So [I read] things that affect me and things that, um, affect a lot of people in general. (P27)
	Funny and entertaining		• I do enjoy humor and I'd like to try to balance that out because there are a lot of stories out there that are not necessarily pleasant. So, just to have a balance in my exposure. (P10) • I just like to read them for entertainment, I guess. (P37)
	Different spin on things		• I usually care about a different spin on what more like think pieces … trying to read stuff that I haven't heard of before. (P50)

Table 3.10 Reasons for Using a Method of Reading News

Reading Method	*Reasons for Using the Method*	*Selected Examples of Participants' Description*
Read the full news story closely	• Interesting and important • Want to know more • Like being informed • A detailed kind of person	• I more often read fully … and that's because I'm not very good at skimming. I am a detailed kind of person. I need every single bit of information to understand. (P15) • If it's informing me of things that I haven't heard of before, I'll try to take more time to really like absorb it. (P50)
Skim the main parts of the news story	• Length of the article • Short on time • Not very interesting/ boring • Writing style	• If it goes-if it's something that's super long and especially if it's something that -maybe the headline piqued my interest and the-my thing was answered in the first few paragraphs but it still goes on and on and on and I'm not that interested in the overall thing, I might skim it then, or if I'm short on time. (P21) • If something is super boring, I'll just look at the headlines and look for a few sentences or read captions of the pictures. (P15)
Scan the headlines/ lead paragraphs	• Not very interesting	• If it's a story that I don't think I would, you know, um, be interested in I simply would just look at the headline and just skip over it. (P18)
Scroll through an entire article first	• Find out the length of the news item	• Sometimes what I'll do is I will scroll through an entire article as soon as I get to it, just to see how long it is. And if it looks to be really long, then I'll just skip it. (P43)

activities. Additional insights about finding behaviors and the finding methods were obtained from the qualitative follow-up interviews.

3.3.1 *News finding behavior*

During the diary study, regarding news finding, participants chose "Not applicable (NA)" for more than half of the news items, which could mean that participants were not engaged in finding those news items. Among 220 news items, 98 news items (44.5%) were found by visiting and searching news sites or news apps, 86 news items (39.1%) were found by checking social media where the news story was posted or discussed, and 33 news items (15.0%) were found by using Google or other search engines; the remaining three news items were found through feeds or notifications (1.4%). Table 3.11 shows the finding behavior of participants.

3.3.1.1 *Demographic differences*

In this section, we discuss the demographic differences in people's news finding behavior. We discovered that there were significant differences among various gender, age group, class type, student type, and major groups. The specific differences are outlined next.

3.3.1.1.1 GENDER

There were statistically significant differences in finding behavior between participants of different genders. Interestingly, regarding

Table 3.11 Participants' Finding Behavior

Finding News (n = 220)	#	%
Visited and searched news site or news apps	98	44.5
Checked social media where the news story was posted/discussed	86	39.1
Used Google or other search engines	33	15.0
Found via notification	3	1.4
Total	220	100.0

finding news, a significantly higher proportion of news stories were found by male participants than by female participants.

3.3.1.1.2 AGE GROUP

There were statistically significant differences in finding behavior among participants in different age groups. A significantly higher proportion of news stories were found by participants who are 20–24 years old than by participants in other age groups.

3.3.1.1.3 CLASS TYPE

There were statistically significant differences in finding behavior among participants in different classes. A significantly higher proportion of news stories were found by junior students than by participants in other class levels.

3.3.1.1.4 STUDENT TYPE

Statistically significant differences were found among student types and sharing. International students shared a significantly higher proportion of news stories than did American students.

3.3.1.1.5 MAJOR

There were statistically significant differences in finding behavior among participants in different majors. A significantly higher proportion of news stories were found by students who had not declared their majors than by arts & humanities students, engineering students, social science students, or science students.

3.3.2 Methods of finding the news

In this section, we discuss the demographic differences in how to find news, i.e., news finding methods. We discovered that there were significant differences among various age groups, ethnicity, classes, and major groups. The specific differences are outlined next.

3.3.2.1 Age group

In terms of specific finding methods, the highest proportion of the age group that "used Google or other search engines" was those who were 25–29 years old. The age group that had the highest proportion of participants who "visited and searched news sites or news app" was people who were 20–24 years old. The age group with the highest proportion of participants who "checked social media where the news story was posted/discussed" was people under 20 years old. The age group with the highest proportion of participants who found news through "notification" was people who were 20–24 years old.

Table 3.12 shows the top three news finding methods for various age groups. As it is clear that for our participants "social media" was a main vehicle to find news, although checking social media for news was only the number 1 news finding method for people who were under 20.

Table 3.12 Top 3 News Finding Methods by Age Groups

Age Group	*Top 1*	*Top 2*	*Top 3*
Under 20	Checked social media where the news story was posted / discussed	Visited and searched news site or news app	Used Google or other search engines
20–24	Visited and searched news site or news app	Checked social media where the news story was posted /discussed	Used Google or other search engines
25–29	Used Google or other search engines	Checked social media where the news story was posted /discussed	Visited and searched news site or news app
30 or above	Visited and searched news site or news app	Checked social media where the news story was posted /discussed	Used Google or other search engines

Table 3.13 Top 3 News Finding Methods by Ethnic Groups

Ethnic Group	*Top 1*	*Top 2*	*Top 3*
American Indian	Visited and searched news site or news app	None	None
Asian	Visited and searched news site or news app	Checked social media where the news story was posted /discussed	Used Google or other search engines
Black/ African American	Visited and searched news site or news app	Used Google or other search engines	None
Hispanic Latino	• Used Google or other search engines • Checked social media where the news story was posted /discussed	Visited and searched news site or news app	
White Caucasian	Checked social media where the news story was posted /discussed	Visited and searched news site or news app	Used Google or other search engines

3.3.2.2 Ethnicity

For news finding, the ethnic group with the highest proportion of participants who "used Google or other search engines" was Hispanic/Latino. The ethnic group with the highest proportion of participants who "visited and searched news site or news app" was American Indian. The ethnic group with the highest proportion of participants who "checked social media where the news story was posted/discussed" was White/Caucasian. And finally, the ethnic group with the highest proportion of participants who found news through "notification" was also White/Caucasian.

Table 3.13 shows the top three news finding methods for various ethnic groups. While ethnic groups such as American Indian, Asian, and Black/African American had "visited and searched news site or news app" as their number one finding method, both Hispanic/Latino and White Caucasian participants checked social media first. Hispanic/Latino participants also used Google or other search engines as their number one news finding method, tied with checking social media for news.

3.3.2.3 Class

For specific news finding methods, the class with the highest proportion of participants who "used Google or other search engines" was doctoral students. The class with the highest proportion of participants who "visited and searched news site or news app" was master's students. The class with the highest proportion of participants who "checked social media where the news story was posted/discussed" was juniors. The class with the highest proportion of participants who found news through "notification" was seniors.

Table 3.14 shows the top three news finding methods for various class levels. While class levels such as freshman, sophomore,

Table 3.14 Top 3 News Finding Methods by Class Levels

Class Levels	*Top 1*	*Top 2*	*Top 3*
Freshman	Checked social media where the news story was posted /discussed	• Used Google or other search engines • Visited and searched news site or news app	
Sophomore	• Visited and searched news site or news app • Checked social media where the news story was posted /discussed	None	None
Junior	Checked social media where the news story was posted /discussed	Visited and searched news site or news app	Used Google or other search engines
Senior	Visited and searched news site or news app	Checked social media where the news story was posted /discussed	Used Google or other search engines

(*Continued*)

Table 3.14 (Continued)

Class Levels	*Top 1*	*Top 2*	*Top 3*
Master's student	Visited and searched news site or news app	Checked social media where the news story was posted /discussed	None
Doctoral student	• Used Google or other search engines • Checked social media where the news story was posted /discussed	Visited and searched news site or news app	

junior, and doctoral students had "Checked social media where the news story was posted /discussed" as their number one news finding method, both senior and master's students used "Visited and searched news site or news app" as their top method. Doctoral students also used Google or other search engines as their number one news finding method, tied with checking social media for news.

3.3.2.4 Major

For news finding methods, the highest proportion of participants who "used Google or other search engines" was majoring in social sciences. The highest proportion of participants who "visited and searched news site or news app" was majoring in engineering. The highest proportion of participants who "checked social media where the news story was posted/discussed" was people with undeclared majors. The highest proportion of participants who found news "through notification" was people with science majors.

Table 3.15 shows the top three news finding methods for various majors or academic interests. While people majoring in sciences or with undeclared majors had "Checked social media where the news story was posted /discussed" as their most common news finding method, people specializing in arts & humanities, social

Table 3.15 Top 3 News Finding Methods by Majors

Majors	*Top 1*	*Top 2*	*Top 3*
Arts & humanities	Visited and searched news site or news app	Checked social media where the news story was posted /discussed	Used Google or other search engines
Sciences	Checked social media where the news story was posted / discussed	Visited and searched news site or news app	Used Google or other search engines
Social sciences	Visited and searched news site or news app	Checked social media where the news story was posted /discussed	Used Google or other search engines
Engineering	Visited and searched news site or news app	Checked social media where the news story was posted /discussed	None
Undeclared	Checked social media where the news story was posted / discussed	Visited and searched news site or news app	None

sciences, and engineering used "Visited and searched news site or news app" as their top news finding method.

3.3.3 Additional insights about finding behavior and methods

Our follow-up interviews provided further insights into participants' news finding behavior, reasons for finding news on their mobile devices, and description of various finding methods.

3.3.3.1 News finding behavior or methods

Participants described their specific news finding behaviors. For finding news via their mobile phones, P21 indicates that "I think there was at least one entry where I saw something on the news and then looked it up on my phone." P31 commented on their getting news from social media: "If I find news on Facebook, I would read that on my phone, most likely." P27 also indicated that "I start with social media first and then eventually, ... so I'll start with social media." P27 also relied on Google for finding news: "I was just using Google and I just found it right there. It was the first thing that popped up." P40, on the other hand, used a news app for finding news: "I found it because I had seen the news, and just kind of deleted it. And then later, I remembered that I had seen it, so I went back into the Times app to find it."

Participants also described how they used their news app or Google to find news. P40 described how they went back to the Times news app to find a news they originally had seen but deleted, "I found it because I had seen the news, and just kind of deleted it. And then later, I remembered that I had seen it, so I went back into the Times app to find it." P37 relied on Google to look up news in a topical area: "I usually go on Google and just look up the topic that I'm interested in." In some cases, participants used both social media and Google for news finding. P27 commented on finding a specific news item: "I got it on Tumblr and then looked for it later through Google."

Two participants used their own laptops to look up breaking news. P31 pointed out "When I say I just read them, that means that I would have found them on my laptop first and then read them on my phone later." P27 discussed how they found the news about the Munich Shooter: "for the Munich shooter thing – on my laptop – because that was sort of important at the time."

3.3.3.2 Reasons for finding news

Most of the participants were motivated to find and search for news because the story was interesting or important. P40 went to search for a news item because "I thought it was interesting. I didn't even know that they were happening right now, I think it's interesting." P27 looked for the news about the Munich Shooter because "that was very important" news at the time. When hearing from their friends or family members mentioning some news stories, participants would go to find them. According to P50, "Whenever I heard people talk about it, I'd be like 'what are you talking about?' and then I just Googled it. And then I would read it." Several participants used their laptops to find news because they found them more user friendly for finding news. As commented by P31, "I think that phones are more convenient than laptops are. I think that laptops are a little more user-friendly than phone."

3.4 Sharing news

3.4.1 News sharing behaviors

In our diary study, among 466 news items, participants shared 103 news items. This showed that about one-fifth of the news items participants entered into the diary were shared. We also found some statistically significant demographic differences in news sharing in terms of age group, ethnicity, class, and student type.

3.4.1.1 Age groups

A significantly higher proportion of news stories were shared by participants who are 25–29 years old than by other age groups. More specifically, among the news entries submitted by each age group, participants who were 25–29 years old reported sharing 32.0% of the news entries, which was the highest proportion when compared to other age groups. Interestingly, the age group of 20–24 years old shared the lowest proportion of their news stories (13.1%).

3.4.1.2 Ethnicity

In terms of ethnicity, a significantly higher proportion of news stories were shared by participants who were American Indian (25%) than by participants who were Asian (22.9%), Black/African American (20.6%), or Hispanic/Latino (20.0%). Interestingly, White/Caucasian participants shared the lowest proportion (11.7%) of the news stories they submitted.

3.4.1.3 School types

For participants coming from a college, university, or other types of higher education institutions, the highest proportion of news was shared by people from institutions other than colleges or universities (33.3%), followed by news shared by participants from a university (22.4%). The proportion of the news shared by participants who were students in a college was the lowest (12.5%).

3.4.1.4 Classes

In terms of various class levels, the highest proportion of news (28.0%) was shared by doctoral students, followed by sophomores (23.9%), then freshmen (20.0%). Interestingly, the lowest proportion of news items was shared by juniors (8.3%) or master's students (7.0%).

3.4.1.5 Student types

Interestingly, our study found that a higher proportion of news items (25.8%) were shared by international students than by American students (15.8%). The fact that there were 10% more news stories shared by students from outside the United States than the US students is rather surprising.

3.4.2 Methods of news sharing

3.4.2.1 Overview of news sharing methods

Among the news items that were shared, participants provided some explanation of how they shared some of the news items ($n = 103$). Among various methods of sharing, the highest proportion of the news items shared (41.7%) were shared through instant messaging (IM) or texting, while the second-highest proportion of the news (36.9%) were shared via social media or blog. There were other sharing methods such as sharing by word of mouth or discussions (9.7%) or sharing through email (6.8%). Participants selected "other" for five news items that were shared (4.9%). Table 3.16 presents various sharing methods.

3.4.2.2 Demographic differences in news sharing methods

There were demographic differences in the news sharing methods in terms of participants' gender, ethnicity, and major. The specific differences are reported in the following sections.

Table 3.16 Participants' News Sharing Methods

Sharing Behavior	#	%
Via instant messaging or texting	43	41.7
Via social media/blog	38	36.9
Via word of mouth/discussion	10	9.7
Via email	7	6.8
Other	5	4.9
Total	103	100.0

Table 3.17 Top 3 News Sharing Methods by Gender

Gender	*Top 1*	*Top 2*	*Top 3*
Female	Via instant messaging or texting	Via social media/blog	Via word of mouth/discussion
Male	Via social media/blog	Via instant messaging or texting	• Via word of mouth/discussion • Via email

3.4.2.2.1 GENDER

In the case of gender, for multiple sharing methods, higher proportions of news items were shared by female participants. These methods included "via other methods" (n = 5, 100%), "via word of mouth/discussion" (n = 7, 70%), "via instant messaging/texting (n = 29, 67.5%)", and "via email" (n = 4, 57.1%). A higher proportion of the news items were shared by male participants "via social media/blog" (n = 22, 57.9%). It is interesting to note that male participants shared more news via social media, whereas female shared via instant messaging/texting, which might be more private than social media. Table 3.17 shows the top three sharing methods by gender. While male participants had social media/blog as their number 1 sharing method, female participants' number 1 method was via IM or texting. For number three, both male and female participants used word of mouth, but sharing via email was tied with sharing through word of mouth as the top 3 method for male participants.

Table 3.18 Top 3 News Sharing Methods by Ethnic Groups

Ethnic Group	*Top 1*	*Top 2*	*Top 3*
American Indian	Via other methods	• Via social media/blog • Via IM or texting • Via word of mouth/discussion	None
Asian	Via social media/blog	Via IM or texting	Via email
Black/African American	Via IM or texting	Via social media/blog	Via word of mouth/discussion
Hispanic Latino	Via IM or texting	• Via social media/blog • Via word of mouth/discussion • Via other methods	None
White Caucasian	Via social media/blog	Via IM or texting	Via word of mouth/discussion

3.4.2.2.2 ETHNICITY

In the case of ethnicity, the highest proportions of news shared "via email" (*n* = 4, 57.1%), "via social media/blog" (*n* = 20, 52.6%), and "via instant messaging/texting" (*n* = 19, 44.2%) were by Asian participants. The only sharing method that had the highest proportion of news shared by White/Caucasian participants was "via word of mouth/discussion" (*n* = 5, 50.0%), and the only sharing method that had the highest proportion of news shared by Hispanic/Latino participants was "via other methods" (*n* = 3, 60.0%). Table 3.18 shows the top three sharing methods within an ethnic group.

3.4.2.2.3 MAJOR

For various majors or specialties, the highest proportions of news shared "via email" (*n* = 3, 42.9%) was by people majoring in engineering. Interestingly, the highest proportion of news shared "via social media/blog" (*n* = 20, 52.6%) or via word of mouth/discussion (*n* = 8, 80.0%) were by people majoring in social sciences. The

Table 3.19 Top 3 News Sharing Methods by Major Groups

Majors	*Top 1*	*Top 2*	*Top 3*
Arts & humanities	Via social media/blog	• Via email • Via other methods	None
Sciences	Via IM or texting	Via social media/blog	Via other methods
Social sciences	Via social media/blog	Via IM or texting	Via word of mouth/ discussion
Engineering	Via social media/blog	• Via email • Via IM or texting	None
Undeclared	Via email	None	None

highest proportion of news shared "via instant messaging/texting" (n = 24, 55.8%) was by people majoring in sciences. The highest proportion of news shared "via other methods" (n = 2, 40.0%) was by people majoring in arts & humanities and sciences. Across various major groups, the top three sharing methods within a group varied. While arts & humanities, social sciences, and engineering majors had "social media/blog" as their number 1 sharing method, sharing "Via IM or Texting" was the number 1 method for people majoring in sciences. In contrast, the only method of sharing for people with undeclared majors was "via email." No other sharing techniques were used by people whose majors had not yet been declared. Table 3.19 shows the top three sharing methods within various major groups.

3.4.3 *The extent of news sharing*

3.4.3.1 Overview of the extent of news sharing

In addition to the news sharing methods, we asked participants about the extent of sharing. When asked about the extent of news sharing, participants chose "NA" for a majority of news items (n = 423, 81.0%). Participants described the extent to which they shared 99 news items. The results showed that about one-third of the news items were shared by only sending the link (n = 29, 29.3%) and another one-third were shared by providing both the link and the participants' own description or summary of the news items (*n* = 29, 29.3%). Sometimes, participants shared news items by only giving their own descriptions or summary of the news (*n* = 12, 12.1%) or by sending screen captures of the news (*n* = 12, 12.1%). Although in fewer cases, sometimes participants shared by offering the full story and the link (*n* = 6, 6.1%) or by providing the headline and the main parts of the story (*n* = 5, 5.1%). Other methods (*n* = 3, 3.0%) included sharing by giving the headline, the main parts of the story and the link, and sending the full story.

3.4.3.2 Demographic differences in the extent of sharing

There were also demographic differences in the extent of sharing news. In particular, there were differences among participants in different age groups, ethnicities, and student types. The specific differences are reported in the following sections.

3.4.3.2.1 AGE GROUP

The age group with the highest proportion of participants who "shared only the link of the news" was those who were 20–24 years old (*n* = 16, 55.2%). The age group with the highest proportion of participants who "shared only their own description summary" was also people who were 20–24 years old (*n* = 8, 66.7%). The age group with the highest proportion of participants who "shared their own description of the news and the link" was also people 20–24 years old (*n* = 19, 65.5%). The age group with the highest proportion of participants who "shared the headline and the main part of the story" was people who were 20–24 years old (*n* = 4, 80.0%). The age group with the highest proportion of participants who "shared the full story" was people 20–24 years old (*n* = 1, 100.0%).

The age groups with the highest proportion of participants who "shared the headline, the main part of the story, and the link" were people 20–24 years old (*n* = 1, 50.0%) and 30 or above (*n* = 1, 50.0%). The age group with the highest proportion of participants who "shared the full story and the link" was people under 20 (*n* = 2, 33.3%) and people who were 30 or above (*n* = 2, 33.3%). The age group with the highest proportion of participants who "shared the screen capture of the news story" was 25–29 years old (n = 7, 58.3%). The age group with the highest proportion of participants who shared news to other extents was people 25–29 years old (n = 2, 66.7%).

3.4.3.2.2 ETHNICITY

For the extent of sharing, the ethnic group with the highest proportion of participants who "shared only the link of the news" (n = 11, 37.9%), "shared only their own description summary" (n = 5, 41.7%), or "shared their own description of the news and the link" (n = 18, 62.1%) was Asian. The ethnic group with the highest proportion of participants who "shared the screen capture of the news story" (n = 8, 66.7%) or "to other extents" (n = 2, 66.7%) was Hispanic/Latino. The ethnic group with the highest proportion of participants who "shared the headline and the main part of the story" were Asian (n = 2, 40.0%) and White/Caucasian (n = 2, 40.0%). The ethnic groups with the highest proportion of participants who "shared the headline, the main part of the story, and the link" were Asian (n = 1, 50.0%) and Black/African American (n = 1, 50.0%). The ethnic group with the highest proportion of participants who "shared the full story" was American Indian (n = 1, 100.0%). The ethnic group with the highest proportion of participants who "shared the full story and the link" was White/Caucasian (n = 3, 50.0%).

3.4.3.2.3 STUDENT TYPE

For the extent of sharing, the student type with the highest proportions of participants who listed various sharing extent, including "shared only the link of the news" (n = 26, 89.7%), "shared only their own description summary" (n = 12, 100.0%), "shared their own description of the news and the link" (n = 16, 55.2%), "shared the screen capture of the news story" (n = 10, 83.3%), "shared the headline and the main part of the story" (n = 4, 80.0%), "shared the headline, the main part of the story, and the link" (n = 2, 100.0%), "shared the full story" (n = 1, 100.0%), "shared the full story and the link" (n = 5, 83.3%), and finally "shared news in other extents" (n = 3, 100.0%) were American.

3.4.4 Additional insights about sharing behavior and methods

Our follow-up interviews provided further insights into participants' news sharing behavior, reasons for sharing news on their mobile devices, and description of various sharing methods.

3.4.4.1 News sharing behavior

During the follow-up interviews, our participants described whom they shared the news stories with, the timing of the sharing, and the attitude toward the sharing. In terms of whom they shared the new items with, participants mentioned three groups of people: Specific individuals, friends, or family members. P31 commented that rather than sharing the news with the general public, they preferred to share them with specific people –

> If I wanted somebody to see something that I had, then I would talk to them specifically about it. I might text them and tell them to go read it, or to show it to them. As opposed to sharing it with the whole crowd.

As an undergraduate student, P13 indicated that she was often sharing the news with a group of students who are friends –

> I'm in a group chat with a few college students or a few of my friends from UT and basically we all are really liberal and none of us like Trump so I thought that was one of the most outrageous things that I had seen that Trump had done, so that's why I shared it.

P37 shared Olympics news with their family because "we always like to talk about what was going on with the Olympics and I decided to share it with my family."

In terms of the timing of news sharing, some participants would share the news items immediately upon learning about the news. According to P06, "Normally if I share something I try to do it right away." Several participants also commented on being careful in terms of what to share and why they choose not to share the news often. P10 pointed out how they were mindful in sharing news on social media: "I have a presence on social media but I'm very particular with what I decide to share." P40 specified that they did not share the news often, except once in a while sharing with their family members: "I just don't really [share news]. I mean if I found something that I thought was interesting or pertinent enough, I might share it with my mother or my sister." P43 also explained why they seldom share the news: "that's just because I don't really like imposing my opinions on other people."

3.4.4.2 Reasons for sharing or not sharing news

Participants also provided reasons for sharing or not sharing certain news. For sharing news, interestingness, relatedness, humor, or outrageousness of the news stories were the common reasons. Some people were motivated to share news because they wanted to obtain more information. In contrast, reasons for not sharing include the assumption that others might not be interested or they might have already heard about it. If it was a negative story, people would avoid sharing it, or they did not like to impose their own feelings or opinions about the news story on others. Table 3.20

Table 3.20 Reasons for Sharing or Not Sharing News

Reasons	*Participant Comments*
Reason for sharing	
Common interests	• If I just post it on my blog, which means I think, some of my friends might be interested in it. (P1) • I think sharing a news item for me is a very personal thing. I think it calls upon some common experience and it's supposed to lead me closer to the other person by creating a more common experience. (P18)
Relatedness	• That's something that resonates personally and academically… . I tend to share things when I have a personal connection with the person I'm sharing with about the specific news story. (P21)
Funny	• If it's something that would affect us or if we think it's funny… . Like some guy says something stupid, we'll usually share that and laugh at it. (P50)

(*Continued*)

Table 3.20 (Continued)

Reasons	*Participant Comments*
Reason for sharing	
Outrageous	• I thought that was one of the most outrageous things that I had seen that Trump had done, so that's why I shared it. (P13)
For follow up discussion	• I want to share it with someone so we can have some follow up activities. Like I remember I shared something about Disneyland or some astronomy news because I think after sharing that we can have some discussion or things like that. (P1) • That's usually my intent when sharing information and that's usually, like, a cause of a conversation. (P26)
At the request	• So it was-my mom couldn't necessarily access them, or find them, really. So she had specifically asked me to send, if I found anything specific to her. That's why I shared them with her. (P27)
Obtain more information	• I wanna read all of it, so that way, I can get that information and be knowledgeable too, if I share it with people. (P50)
Reasons for not sharing	
Others not interested	• It's only of particular interest to me. And while I'm sure other individuals share it, I don't really feel like spamming my Facebook friends with this stuff that they may or may not care about. (P10)
Others might have heard about it	• If I found something that I thought was interesting or pertinent enough, I might share it with my mother or my sister. But usually these are things that wouldn't interest them or they've already heard about them. (P40)
Stories are political	• I try to stay away from politics. (P6)
Negative stories	• At that time there were so many tragedies and I don't want to share it to just make it worse. (P1)
Not imposing opinions	• I never share stories, like ever. And that's just because I don't really like imposing my opinions on other people. (P43)
Reservation about social media for sharing news	• I just don't really like participating in that kind of environment [Facebook comments about news]. So if it's like a really funny news story or entertainment story that I would be interested in talking about with my friends. I don't really have these kinds of conversations on social media. (P43)

shows various reasons for sharing or not sharing, as well as selected comments from the participants on a specific reason.

3.4.4.3 News sharing methods

Participants reported and described a variety of news sharing methods, ranging from sharing the screenshot, sharing the link, sharing by talking with others, sharing via texting, IM, or chat, posting on personal blog, sharing via email, sharing via phone, or sharing through social media. Participants also reported whether they shared the news with their own summary or comments or without any comments.

Multiple participants preferred sharing a news story through sharing a screenshot. P14 commented, "I would usually share a screen cap if it was like something crazy and something funny." P1 used the sharing of screenshots as their primary method because "everyone is very smart and if they're interested in the title, they can search it by themselves and also if I share a screenshot, which means maybe they can have a basic concept of what I want to say." Both P1 and P6 also tended to share a news story through sending the link. P1 indicated that "If I want to share it with some specific ones, I will use a link because I want him or her to read it totally so we can have some further discussion." P6 also described their way of sharing: "I'll copy the link and then either text it to the person or email it to them." Sharing through instant messaging or chat was another frequently used method, as P6 explained, "Usually I just text during the day … I will just copy and paste the link there, and we kind of discuss things there. Most of the time it's through texting or through that Facebook chat." P37 also commented on how texting could create opportunities for further discussion with their family members: "I find just texting them is much more faster – my parents just put their own perspective as well, so we can just have our own conversation." Sharing verbally was another method. Both P1 and P21 shared specific news stories verbally with their loved ones. P1 talked to her husband about the news of the "Bangladesh attack" and P21 shared with her fiance "verbally and visually" about a news story in Hong Kong.

Other sharing platforms included email, phone, personal blogs, or social media tools. P18 indicated that "the phone definitely makes it a lot easier to share things." P21 occasionally would share news stories in an email. P14 relies on Facebook messenger to share news stories, because they didn't want to "put things on Facebook and Twitter for public exposure." P6, nevertheless, would use Facebook chat for sharing news items. P1, on the other hand, posted news stories "on my blog, which means I think, some of my friends might be interested in."

Some of the participants would share a news story with their own summaries or comments, while others would not include any comments. P37 says that "I just took the story and I just gave them the gist of what was going on, just gave them the gist of the story." P15 would normally add their own comments because "I am pretty opinionated and I always give my two cents." There were also people who typically shared a news story without incorporating their own interpretation and discussion. P6 would wait until their recipient read the news, then probably add their own comments: "Usually I just send the link itself. If I have extra commentary, it usually isn't until after the person has read it." P26 indicates how not sharing their own comments is because their personality being "more of a 'share other people's voices than actually raising my own' kind of person. Especially with the people that I talked to about this article." P43 also linked the fact that she refrains from commenting to her personality,

> I'm a very passive person, and I never write comments on social media about this kind of stuff. Not even just sharing articles about anything, if someone will make a comment on a very charged comment that is controversial, I won't comment on it at all.

3.4.4.4 Reasons for choosing a news sharing method

Our participants also disclosed the reasons that they shared news using a particular method. Both P1 and P6 indicated that they shared their news stories with different groups of people based on the news content. P6 explained that for "a lot of the science articles, I will share with colleagues ... The political stuff is more for family and friends." Multiple participants commented on why they would share a screenshot of the news story. P1 preferred to share the screenshot because they knew if the recipients were interested in the title, "they can search it by themselves" and by sharing a screenshot, "maybe they can have a basic concept of what I want to say." P14, on the other hand, typically shared a screen capture when the news story was "something crazy and something funny."

Participants also described their reasons for sharing the links of a news story, or via instant messaging or chat, or via phone. Convenience and ease are repeatedly mentioned reason. As pointed out by P18, "So usually with an app like WhatsApp or messaging or WeChat or something. It's really easy … the phone definitely makes it a lot easier to share things." P18 also mentioned the immediate impact of news sharing: "So if you want a more immediate impact on your close friends, I think using a phone is really useful for making the impact." Several participants also indicated that their reason for news sharing is to trigger further discussion on the event or make it more personal by adding their own summaries. P1 claimed that using the link to the news story would have the recipient reading the story in its entirety so as to have more discussion: "If I want to share it with some specific ones, I will use a link because I want him or her to read it totally so we can have some further discussion." P18 believes that sharing news is "a very personal thing," so instead of just sharing the link to a news story, P18 would share some comments or summary of the news story. The participant further explains, "I think it calls upon some common experience and it's supposed to lead me closer to the other person by creating more common experience and so I think to just share a link would be too impersonal."

3.5 Storing news

3.5.1 News storing behaviors

In our diary study, among 466 news items submitted by our participants, only 56 (10.7%) were actually stored or saved, indicating that storing news is not a common consumption activity among participants compared to other news consumption activities. Our follow-up interviews further supported this finding. When asked whether they store/save the news stories, participants responded "I didn't store a lot" (P1) and "I don't do it that often" (P6).

For participants who stored news items, they did so in a variety of different ways. The results of our statistical analyses showed

Table 3.21 Participants' News Storing Methods

News Storing Methods	*n*	*%*
By saving the screen capture of the news story	29	51.79
By saving the link to the story	16	28.57
By copying and pasting the news story to a memo or document app	7	12.50
By bookmarking by using the app	3	5.36
Other	1	1.79
Total	56	100.0

that a significantly higher proportion of news items were stored by participants who are 25–29 years old (44.0%) than by other age groups. In addition, a significantly higher proportion of news stories were stored by Hispanic/Latino participants (16.5%) than by Asian participants (6.3%), Caucasian/White participants (6.1%), or Black/African American and American Indian participants (0.0%).

When storing news, the most common way was saving the screen capture of the news story (n = 29, 51.79%), followed by saving the link to the story (n = 16, 28.57%). Table 3.21 displays different ways used by participants in storing news via their smartphones.

3.5.2 Demographic differences in how to store news

We also found statistically significant demographic differences in how to store news in terms of gender, age group, ethnicity, school, class, and major.

3.5.2.1 Gender

In terms of gender differences, interestingly, when news items were stored by "saving the screen capture of the news story," there were more news items saved by female participants (n = 16, 55.2%) than by male participants. Meanwhile, in the case of the news items that were stored by "saving the link to the story," there were more items saved by female participants (n = 11, 68.8%) than by male participants. The news items that were saved by "using other methods to store news" also had more items saved by female participants (n = 1, 100.0%) than male participants. Furthermore, the news items that were saved by "bookmarking by using the app" also had more items saved by female participants (n = 3, 100.0%) than male participants. The only case where there were more male participants than female participants is when it comes to news items that were stored by "copying and pasting the news story to a memo or document app." In this case, more news items were saved by male participants (n = 6, 85.7%) than female participants. Within each gender category, however, the number 1 method of storing was "Save the screen capture of the news story." The top 2 and 3 methods of story vary by gender (see Table 3.22).

3.5.2.2 Age group

There were also age differences in how participants stored news. There were more news stories saved by those who were 20–24 years old than by participants in other age groups for most of the storing methods. These included "saving the link to the story" (n = 11, 68.8%), "copying and pasting the news story to a memo or document app" (n = 7, 100.0%), "bookmaking by the app" (n = 3, 100.0%), and "using other methods" (n = 1, 100.0%). The only method that was used by another age group was "saving the screen capture of the news story," so that the highest number of news stories was saved by this method by those who were 25–29 years old (n = 13, 44.8%).

Table 3.22 Participants' Top News Storing Methods by Gender

Gender	*Top 1*	*Top 2*	*Top 3*
Female	Save the screen capture of the news story	Save the link to the story	• Copy and paste the news story to a memo/document app • Other
Male	Save the screen capture of the news story	Copy and paste the news story to a memo/ document app	Save the link to the story

Table 3.23 Participants' Top News Storing Methods by Age Groups

Age Groups	*Top 1*	*Top 2*	*Top 3*
Under 20	Save the link to the story	Save the screen capture of the news story	
20–24 years	Save the link to the story	Copy and paste the news story to a memo/ document app	• Save the screen capture of the news story • Bookmarked by the app
25–29 years	Save the screen capture of the news story		
30 or above	Save the screen capture of the news story		

Within each age group, however, the number 1 method of storing included "saving the link to the story" for two age groups or "saving the screen capture of the news story" for the two remaining age groups. The top 2 and 3 methods of story vary by age groups (see Table 3.23).

3.5.2.3 Ethnicity

When it comes to ethnicity, differences were found in the storing methods used by Asian, Hispanic Latino, and White/Caucasian participants. There were more news stories saved by Asian participants than by other ethnic groups that stored the news by "saving the link to the story" (n = 8, 50.0%) and by "copying and pasting the news story to a memo or document app" (n = 6, 85.7%). There were more news stories saved by White/ Caucasian participants than by other groups who stored news by "bookmarking by the app" (n = 3, 100.0%) and by "using other methods to store news" (n = 1, 100.0%). Then, there were more news stories saved by Hispanic/Latino participants by "saving the screen capture of the news story" (n = 14, 48.3%).

Within each ethnic group, the number 1 storing method varied: While both Hispanic and Caucasian participants had

Table 3.24 Participants' Top News Storing Methods by Ethnic Groups

Ethnic Groups	*Top 1*	*Top 2*	*Top 3*
Asian	Save the link to the story	Copy and paste the news story to a memo/ document app	Save the screen capture of the news story
Hispanic Latino	Save the screen capture of the news story	Save the link to the story	Copy and paste the news story to a memo/ document app
White Caucasian	Save the screen capture of the news story	Save the link to the story	Bookmarked by the app

"saving the screen capture of the news story" as their number 1 method, Asian participants used "saving the link to the story" as their top method. The top 2 and 3 storage methods also vary by ethnic groups (see Table 3.24).

3.5.2.4 School types

There were differences based on school type (i.e., universities vs colleges) as well. On the one hand, there were more news stories saved by participants from universities who stored the news by "saving the screen capture of the news story" (n = 23, 79.3%), by "saving the link to the story" (n = 9, 56.3%), and by "copying and pasting the news story to a memo or document app" (n = 6, 85.7%). On the other hand, there were more news items stored by participants from colleges who stored the news by "bookmarking by the app" (n = 3, 100.0%) and by "using other methods" (n = 1, 100.0%).

Within each school type, the number 1 storage method varied: While students from colleges had "saving the link to the story" as their top method, university students' top choice was "saving the screen capture of the news story." The top 2 and 3 methods of story also vary by school types (see Table 3.25).

Table 3.25 Participants' Top News Storing Methods by School Types

School Types	*Top 1*	*Top 2*	*Top 3*
College	Save the link to the story	Save the screen capture of the news story	Bookmarked by the app
University	Save the screen capture of the news story	Save the link to the story	Copy and paste the news story to a memo/ document app

3.5.2.5 Class

Statistically significant differences were also found among participants in different classes. Specifically, more news stories were stored by "saving the screen capture of the news story" (n = 17, 56.6%), "saving the link to the story" (n = 8, 50.0%), and by "copying and pasting the news story to a memo or document app" (n = 6, 85.7%) by seniors than by other groups. In the case of saving the news by "bookmarking by the app," the highest proportion of participants who used this storing method were juniors (n = 3, 100.0%). The class that saved more news by "using other methods to store news" than other groups was doctoral students (n = 1, 100.0%).

Within each class level, the number 1 storing method varied: While freshmen, seniors, and doctoral students had "saving the screen capture of the news story" as their number 1 storing method, sophomores' and master's students' choice was "saving the link to the story." Meanwhile, juniors had used "bookmarked by the app" as their top storing method. The top 2 and 3 methods of story also vary by class levels (see Table 3.26). For several class levels, the majority of the participants in that group selected the same methods, leaving no one selecting other methods, and therefore no top 3 or top 2 methods.

3.5.2.6 Major

Lastly, there were differences in how participants stored news among students in different majors. More news stories were stored

Table 3.26 Participants' Top News Storing Methods by Class Levels

Class Levels	*Top 1*	*Top 2*	*Top 3*
Freshman	Save the screen capture of the news story	Save the link to the story	
Sophomore	Save the link to the story		
Junior	Bookmarked by the app	Save the link to the story	Copy and paste the news story to a memo/document app
Senior	Save the screen capture of the news story	Save the link to the story	Copy and paste the news story to a memo/document app
Master's student	Save the link to the story		
Doctoral student	Save the screen capture of the news story		

by "saving the screen capture of the news story" (n = 23, 79.3%), and by "using other methods to store news" (n = 1, 100.0%) by social science students. More news stories were stored by "saving the link to the story" by science students (n = 9, 56.3%), by "copying and pasting the news story to a memo or document app" by engineering students (n = 6, 85.7%), and by "bookmarking by the app" by arts & humanities students (n = 3, 100.0%).

Within each major domain area, the number 1 storage method varied: While students majoring in arts & humanities and social sciences had "saving the screen capture of the news story" as their number 1 storing method, science students' choice was "saving the link to the story," and engineering students' top storing method was "copying and pasting the news story to a memo/document app." Meanwhile, arts & humanities students used "bookmarked by the app" as their top storing methods, tied with "saving the screen capture of the news story." The top 2 and 3 methods of story also vary by majors (see Table 3.27).

Table 3.27 Participants' Top News Storing Methods by Majors

Majors	*Top 1*	*Top 2*	*Top 3*
Arts & humanities	• Save the screen capture of the news story • Bookmarked by the app	Save the link to the story	
Sciences	Save the link to the story	Save thc screen capture of the news story	
Social sciences	Save the screen capture of the news story	Save the link to the story	
Engineering	Copy and paste the news story to a memo/ document app	Save the link to the story	Save the screen capture of the news story

3.5.3 Additional insights about storing behavior and methods

Our follow-up interviews provided further insights into participants' news storing behavior, reasons for storing news on their mobile devices, and description of various storing methods.

3.5.3.1 Regular news storing behavior

Compared with other news consumption activities, news storing is not necessarily a frequently practiced activity. Several participants indicated that they didn't store news often. For instance, P1 stated that "I didn't store a lot," and P6 commented "I never really – I don't do it that often." P6 further indicated that occasionally she would store the screenshot, then delete the photo at a later time: "I [normally keep these screenshots] until I get to the article. Once I get to them again, then I get rid of the photo." P50 claimed that they stored the news sometimes: "I do it sometimes. If the header really catches my eye, I'll try to save it that way. Sometimes I also go back to where I messaged my boyfriend, go back and see other articles that I liked."

3.5.3.2 Reasons for storing news items

The interviews revealed several reasons for storing news items. News items were often stored for possible future use. For instance, one of the participants said, "I saved that one because I think maybe later in some paper I'm writing, I can use that as [a] piece of information or reference things" (P1). Another participant stated that "If it has links to other stuff that I'm interested [in], then, I'll do that or if it has a video that I want to watch in it, and then I'll save it too." Participants also stored news items when the news items were long or seemed to contain a lot of information to read them later. For example, P6 said,

> It was a very thick article, it had a lot of information and I kind of skimmed through it and I wasn't able to give it the attention that I wanted to. So I took the snapshot, it'll be like a reminder that I want to go back to this one.

In a similar vein, P50 stated, "Sometimes I'll store it especially [if] it is a really long article, I'll just store it so I can read the rest of it later." In other cases, people stored a news story to share it with another person. For example, P6 said, "Then other times, I'll store them for people who I think might be interested in them."

Same as what P1 commented on using the news story for paper writing, P50 also connected storing news with her learning and classes: "If it's something that's more in-depth like theoretical or current events, social justice, I am in a class that's about women's gender and sexuality, I'll bring it up to my professor sometimes." Similar to specific areas of learning, participants also stored news items to pursue further readings or other related interesting readings. P50 indicated that she would sometimes go back to see whether there were other articles that she liked. She continued, "If it has links to other stuff that I'm interested [in], then I'll do that or if it has a video that I want to watch in it, then I'll save it too."

3.6 Summary

In this chapter, we provide a detailed account of each of the news consumption activities, starting from receiving or noticing news items, to news finding, news reading, news sharing, and news storing. We describe the behavioral patterns for specific news consumption activities, followed by statistically significant demographic differences in a given activity. These include differences in gender, age groups, ethnicity, students' academic status and academic interests, and how they affect a particular consumption activity. We then present further insights based on participants' comments in the follow-up interviews. In this manner, we provide a comprehensive understanding of each consumption activity at a depth that has seldom been explored in existing literature.

4 Mobile News Reactions

Evaluative Reactions, Affective Reactions

4.1 Use of semantic differential scales for gauging people's evaluative and affective reactions to news

When consuming news, people may have different reactions to stories. In our diary study, we used semantic differential scales to capture participants' evaluative and affective reactions to each of the news items they submitted for the study. Semantic differential scales use "a pair of antonyms, which are usually two adjectives (e.g., difficult-easy; constrained-free)" (Verhagen, van den Hooff, & Meents, 2015, p. 110). These scales can be binary point scales or multi-point scales; multi-point scales are usually used for more complex concepts. Using semantic differential scales is a common method of measuring people's thoughts and feelings toward specific concepts, objects, or events.

In our study, we used 12 evaluative adjective pairs and 11 affective adjective pairs to examine participants' various reactions to news items. These pairs were developed based on the analysis of previous studies that used semantic differential scales (Ajzen & Timkoe, 1986; Osgood, Suci, & Tannenbaum, 1957; Purcell, Rainie, Mitchell, & Rosenstiel, 2010; Scott, 1967; Tang, Ng, Strzalkowski, & Kantor, 2003). We used binary scales rather than multi-point scales to make it easier and quicker for the participants to indicate their reactions for each of the news items they submitted.

In this chapter, we describe the semantic differential scales we used in our study, report the reactions participants had for different types of news, and share significant demographic differences in how participants reacted to news. In addition,

DOI: 10.4324/9781003053002-4

based on the post-diary follow-up interviews, we further describe participants' different reactions to news, such as their reasons for choosing certain evaluative and affective reactions. We also explain why participants sometimes had seemingly conflicting reactions to the same news.

4.1.1 Bipolar adjective pairs for evaluative reactions

In order to examine participants' evaluative reactions, we asked, "How would you evaluate this news story?" and asked them to check one answer from each binary scale. Then, 12 adjective pairs were provided. The adjective pairs provided to the participants are displayed in Table 4.1.

4.1.2 Bipolar adjective pairs for affective reactions

In the case of participants' affective reactions to news, we asked participants to "Describe your emotional reaction to this news story by choosing one term that best represents your reaction from the following binary scales." Then, 11 adjective pairs were provided. The affective pairs we provided are presented in Table 4.2.

Table 4.1 Adjective Pairs for Evaluative Reactions

Evaluative Pairs
Deep ---- Shallow
Valuable ---- Worthless
Heavy ---- Light
Clear ---- Hazy
Sharp ---- Dull
Honest ---- Dishonest
Fresh ---- Stale
Fair ---- Unfair
Wide ---- Narrow
Beneficial ---- Harmful
Beautiful ---- Ugly
Good ---- Bad

Table 4.2 Adjective Pairs for Affective Reactions

Affective Pairs
Strong ---- Weak
Calm ---- Agitated
Pleasant ---- Unpleasant
Happy ---- Sad
Peaceful ---- Ferocious
Relaxed ---- Tense
Nice ---- Awful
Bright ---- Dark
Smooth ---- Rough
Comfortable ---- Uncomfortable
Pleasurable ---- Painful

4.2 Evaluative reactions

4.2.1 Evaluative reactions to news

Among the 522 diary entries, there were more news items that were evaluated as deep (55.0%, n = 287) than shallow (45.0%, n = 235), valuable (78.9%, n = 412) than worthless (21.1%, n = 110), heavy (51.3%, n = 268) than light (48.7%, n = 254), clear (82.8%, n = 432) than hazy (17.2%, n = 90), sharp (75.7%, n = 395) than dull (24.3%, n = 127), honest (91.8%, n = 479) than dishonest (8.2%, n = 43), fresh (84.7%, n = 442) than stale (15.3%, n = 80), fair (82.0%, n = 428) than unfair (18.0%, n = 94), narrow (58.2%, n = 304) than wide (41.8%, n = 218), beneficial (82.0%, n = 428) than harmful (18.0%, n = 94), beautiful (58.4%, n = 305) than ugly (41.6%, n = 217), and good (59.2%, n = 309) than bad (40.8%, n = 213). Overall, there were more positive evaluative reactions than negative reactions. The wide–narrow semantic differential pair was the only one that had more negative reactions (i.e., narrow) than positive reactions (i.e., wide).

4.2.2 Variations of evaluative reactions by types of news

We found some statistically significant differences in participants' evaluative reactions to different types of news. In other words, different types of news had different proportions of items that were regarded as deep rather than shallow, valuable rather than worthless, heavy rather than light, sharp rather than dull, honest rather than dishonest, fresh rather than stale, beneficial rather than harmful, beautiful rather than ugly, or good rather than bad. There were no significant differences in the proportions of news that were regarded as clear rather than hazy, fair rather than unfair, or wide rather than narrow.

4.2.2.1 Deep vs shallow

On the one hand, there were significantly higher proportions of the following types of news that were more often regarded as deep than as shallow. These types of news include environmental news (75%), financial news (72.7%), commentary and opinion news (71.4%), public health news (71.4%), science and technology news (62.5%), society news (62.0%), and political news (59.0%). On the other hand, significantly higher proportions of the following types of news were more often regarded as shallow than as deep: Sports news (70.8%), consumer news (70.0%), entertainment news (68.0%), education news (62.5%), and other news (57.1%).

4.2.2.2 Valuable vs worthless

There were different proportions of news items that were regarded as valuable than as worthless based on the types of news. More specifically, environmental news (93.8%), consumer news (90.0%), science and technology news (87.5%), commentary and opinion news (85.7%), public health news (85.7%), political news (82.5%), society news (81.5%), education news (75.0%), financial news (72.7%), other news (71.4%), sports news (68.8%), and entertainment news (54.0%) were more often regarded as valuable than as worthless.

4.2.2.3 Heavy vs light

The following types of news had significantly higher proportions of news items that were regarded as heavy than as light: Commentary and opinion news (66.7%), society news (65.2%), financial news (63.6%), political news (62.8%), environmental news (62.5%), and public health news (61.9%). On the contrary, significantly higher proportions of the following types of news were regarded as light than as heavy: Consumer news (80.0%), education news (75.0%), science and technology news (75.0%), entertainment news (72.0%), sports news (70.8%), and other news (64.3%).

4.2.2.4 Sharp vs dull

The following types of news had significantly higher proportions of items that were regarded as sharp than as dull: Public health news (90.5%), society news (84.8%), financial news (81.8%), political news (81.4%), science and technology news (77.1%), education news (75.0%), commentary and opinion news (71.4%), consumer news (70.0%), environmental news (68.8%), sports news (58.3%), other news (57.1%), and entertainment news (56.0%).

4.2.2.5 Honest vs dishonest

There were significantly higher proportions of news items that were regarded as honest than as dishonest. These included consumer news (100.0%), environmental news (100.0%), financial news (100.0%), science and technology news (100.0%), other news (100.0%), society news (95.7%), sports news (93.8%), public health news (90.5%), political news (88.0%), entertainment news (86.0%), commentary and opinion news (85.7%), and education news (75.0%).

4.2.2.6 Fresh vs stale

A significantly higher proportion of news items were regarded as fresh than as stale. This was true across the following types of news: Public health news (95.2%), society news (91.3%), political news (88.5%), science and technology news (85.4%), financial news (81.8%), environmental news (81.3%), consumer news (80.0%), sports news (79.2%), other news (78.6%), education news (75.0%), commentary and opinion news (71.4%), and entertainment news (70.0%).

4.2.2.7 Beneficial vs harmful

The following types of news had significantly higher proportions of items that were regarded as beneficial than as harmful: Financial news (100%), other news (100%), science and technology news (95.8%), public health news (95.2%), consumer news (90.0%), education news (87.5%), environmental news (87.5%), commentary and opinion news (85.7%), society news (79.3%), political news (78.7%), entertainment news (76.0%), and sports news (70.8%).

4.2.2.8 Beautiful vs ugly

There were many types of news that had significantly higher proportions of items that were regarded as beautiful than as ugly. These included consumer news (80.0%), public health news (76.2%), science and technology news (75.0%), commentary and opinion news (71.4%), entertainment news (64.0%), education news (62.5%), sports news (62.5%), other news (57.1%), financial news (54.5%), and political news (53.6%). On the other hand, significantly higher proportions of news items of the following types were regarded as ugly than as beautiful: Environmental news (56.3%) and society news (52.2%).

4.2.2.9 Good vs bad

The following types of news had significantly higher proportions of items that were regarded as good than as bad: Consumer news (90.0%), education news (87.5%), financial news (81.8%), science and technology news (79.2%), other news (78.6%), commentary and opinion news (76.2%), public health news (76.2%), entertainment news (72.0%), and sports news (66.7%). On the other hand, significantly higher proportions of news items of the following types were regarded as bad than as good: Environmental news (68.8%), political news (53.0%), and society news (47.8%).

4.2.3 Variations of evaluative reactions by demographic attributes

Our statistical analyses showed several interesting demographic differences in participants' evaluative reactions to news. In the case of gender, on the one hand, a significantly higher proportion of female participants (81.7%) viewed the news as more valuable than worthless than male participants (72.7%). On the other hand, a higher proportion of male participants (88.2%) evaluated news as more fair than unfair as compared with female participants (79.2%), showing that female participants had more positive evaluative reactions to news than male students.

Participants in different age groups also had significantly different evaluative reactions to the news. Higher proportions of participants who were under 20 (71.7%), 20–24 years old (52.3%), and 30 years or above (76.6%) evaluated news as more narrow than wide, while those who were 25–29 years old (68%) evaluated news as wide.

In addition, participants with different ethnicities had significantly different evaluative reactions to the news, so there were different proportions of participants who viewed the news as sharp rather than dull. More specifically, 82.4% of Black/African American participants, 80.2% of Caucasian participants, 73.6% of Asian participants, 66.7% of American Indian participants, and 64.7% of Hispanic participants viewed news items as sharp. There were also different proportions of participants who evaluated news as fresh rather than stale. More specifically, 94.1% of Black/African American participants, 85.8% of Caucasian participants, 84.7% of Hispanic participants, 82.6% of Asian participants, and 58.3% of American Indian participants viewed news items as fresh. Thus, higher proportions of Black/African American and Caucasian participants had positive evaluative reactions to news than other participants.

Participants from different classes also had significantly different evaluative reactions to the news, so there were different proportions of participants who viewed the news as sharp rather than dull. More specifically, 90.0% of junior participants, 80.4% of sophomore participants, 80.0% of doctoral student participants, 75.0% of freshman participants, 71.0% of senior participants, and 69.8% of master's student participants viewed news items as sharp. In addition, a higher proportion of junior participants (65.0%) and master's student participants (51.2%) evaluated news as wide than as narrow, while a higher proportion of sophomore participants (76.1%), freshman participants (68.3%), senior participants (58.8%), and doctoral student participants (61.3%) evaluated news as narrow.

There were multiple significant differences between participants who are American students and those who are international students. Significantly higher proportions of international students viewed news as fair than as unfair, as compared with American students. More specifically, 92.4% of international student participants and 80.5% of American student participants viewed news items as fair, whereas 19.5% of American student participants and 7.6% of international student participants viewed news items as unfair. Meanwhile, significantly higher proportions of international students viewed news items as wide than as narrow, as compared with American students. More specifically, 53.0% of international student participants and 40.1% of American student participants viewed news items as wide, whereas 59.9% of American student participants and 47.0% of international student participants viewed news items as narrow. In addition, significantly higher proportions of international students viewed news as beneficial than as harmful, as compared with American students. More specifically, 90.9% of international student participants and 80.7% of American student participants viewed news items as beneficial, whereas 19.3% of American student participants and 9.1% of international student participants viewed news items as harmful. Meanwhile, significantly higher proportions of international students viewed news as beautiful than as ugly, as compared with American students. More specifically, 71.2% of international student participants and 56.6% of American student participants viewed news items as beautiful, whereas 53.4% of American student participants and 28.8% of international student participants viewed news items as ugly, indicating that international students had more positive evaluative reactions to news than did American students.

There were also multiple significant differences among participants in different majors in their evaluative reactions to news. More specifically, 100% of participants with undeclared majors, 83.8% of science participants, 78.3% of social science participants, 76.7% of arts & humanities participants, and 64.9% of engineering participants viewed news items as valuable rather than worthless. Interestingly, a higher proportion of arts & humanities participants (59.2%) evaluated news items as light rather than heavy, while a higher proportion of participants with undeclared majors (75%), science participants (58.1%), engineering participants (56.8%), and social science participants (50.7%) evaluated news items as heavy than as light. In addition, there were different proportions of participants with different majors who viewed news items as clear rather than hazy. More specifically, 100% of participants with undeclared majors, 87.5% of arts & humanities participants, 82.9% of social science participants, 81.6% of science participants, and 61.9% of engineering participants viewed news as clear. There were also different proportions of students who viewed news items as honest rather than dishonest. More specifically, 100% of participants with undeclared majors, 94.1% of science participants, 92.5% of arts & humanities participants, 92.2% of social science participants, and 75.7% of engineering participants viewed news items as honest. There were also different proportions of participants with different majors who viewed news items as fresh rather than stale. More specifically, 100% of participants with undeclared majors, 91.9% of science participants, 82.0% of social science participants, 81.1% of engineering participants, and 57.5% of arts & humanities participants assessed news items as fresh rather than stale. Interestingly, a higher proportion of engineering participants (59.5%) evaluated news items as wide than as narrow, while a higher proportion of social science participants (65.9%), arts & humanities participants (57.5%), and science participants (52.2%) viewed news items as narrow. In the case of participants with undeclared majors, there were equal proportions of participants (50%) who viewed news items as wide or narrow. There were different proportions of participants who viewed news items as beneficial or harmful. More specifically, 100% of participants with undeclared majors, 88.3% of arts & humanities participants, 81.6% of social science participants, 79.4% of science participants, and 67.6% of engineering participants viewed news items as beneficial rather than harmful.

4.3 Affective reactions

4.3.1 Affective reactions to news

Among the 522 diary entries, there were more news items that were evaluated as strong (59.0%, $n = 308$) than weak (41.0%, $n = 214$), calm (61.1%, $n = 319$) than agitated (38.9%, $n = 203$), pleasant (53.4%, $n = 279$) than unpleasant (46.6%, $n = 243$), happy (51.1%,

$n = 267$) than sad (48.9%, $n = 255$), peaceful (65.3%, $n = 341$) than ferocious (34.7%, $n = 181$), relaxed (58.2%, $n = 304$) than tense (41.8%, $n = 218$), nice (58.0%, $n = 303$) than awful (42.0%, $n = 219$), bright (54.8%, $n = 286$) than dark (45.2%, $n = 236$), smooth (56.5%, $n = 295$) than rough (43.5%, $n = 227$), comfortable (57.1%, $n = 298$) than uncomfortable (42.9%, $n = 224$), and pleasurable (56.9%, $n = 297$) than painful (43.1%, $n = 225$). Overall, there were more positive affective reactions than negative reactions.

4.3.2 *Variations of affective reactions by types of news*

We also analyzed whether there are statistically significant differences in participants' affective reactions to different types of news. We found that there were different proportions of news items that were regarded as strong rather than weak, calm rather than agitated, pleasant rather than unpleasant, happy rather than sad, peaceful rather than ferocious, relaxed rather than tense, nice rather than awful, bright rather than dark, smooth rather than rough, comfortable rather than uncomfortable, or pleasurable rather than painful, depending on the types of news.

4.3.2.1 Strong vs weak

There were significantly higher proportions of news that were regarded as strong than as weak. These types of news were public health news (71.4%), political news (67.8%), society news (64.1%), commentary and opinion news (61.9%), and science and technology news (52.1%). Significantly higher proportions of the following types of news were regarded as weak than as strong: Education news (62.5%), consumer news (60.0%), sports news (56.3%), financial news (54.5%), and entertainment news (52.0%). In addition, two types of news were split 50/50 between strong and weak: Other news (50%) and environmental news (50%).

4.3.2.2 Calm vs agitated

There were significantly higher proportions of the following types of news that were regarded as calm than as agitated: Education news (100.0%), other news (92.9%), science and technology news (83.3%), consumer news (80.0%), public health news (76.2%), sports news (72.9%), entertainment news (72.0%), commentary and opinion news (66.7%), financial news (63.6%), and society news (51.1%). On the other hand, significantly higher proportions of the following types of news were regarded as agitated than as calm: Environmental news (62.5%) and political news (51.4%).

4.3.2.3 Pleasant vs unpleasant

Significantly higher proportions of the following types of news that were regarded as pleasant than as unpleasant: Education news (87.5%), financial news (81.8%), consumer news (80.0%), science and technology news (75.0%), other news (71.4%), commentary and opinion news (71.4%), public health news (71.4%), entertainment news (66.0%), and sports news (56.3%). On the other hand, significantly higher proportions of the following types of news were regarded as unpleasant than as pleasant: Environmental news (68.8%), society news (59.8%), and political news (57.9%).

4.3.2.4 Happy vs sad

There were significantly higher proportions of news items that were perceived as happy than as sad. This was true across the following types of news: Consumer news (80.0%), education news (75.0%), financial news (72.7%), science and technology news (70.8%), other news (64.3%), public health news (61.9%), sports news (58.3%), entertainment news (56.0%), and commentary and opinion news (52.4%). Significantly higher proportions of the following types of news were perceived as sad than as happy: Environmental news (81.3%), society news (59.8%), and political news (55.2%).

4.3.2.5 Peaceful vs ferocious

There were significantly higher proportions of the following types of news that were regarded as peaceful than as ferocious: Consumer news (90.0%), education news (87.5%), science and technology news (83.3%), commentary and opinion news (81.0%), entertainment news (80.0%), public health news (76.2%), financial news (72.7%), other news (71.4%), sports news (70.8%), society news (55.4%), and political news (55.2%). In addition, environmental news was split 50/50 between peaceful and ferocious.

4.3.2.6 Relaxed vs tense

Significantly higher proportions of the following types of news were perceived as relaxed than as tense: Consumer news (80.0%), entertainment news (78.0%), education news (75.0%), science and technology news (72.9%), commentary and opinion news (71.4%), other news (71.4%), sports news (70.8%), financial news (63.6%), and public health news (61.9%). Significantly higher proportions of the following types of news were perceived as tense than as relaxed: Political news (54.1%) and society news (51.1%). In addition, environmental news (50%) was split 50/50 between relaxed and tense.

4.3.2.7 Nice vs awful

There were significantly higher proportions of the following types of news that were regarded as nice than as awful: Consumer news (80.0%), other news (78.6%), science and technology news (77.1%), education news (75.0%), entertainment news (74.0%), financial news (72.7%), commentary and opinion news (71.4%), sports news (68.8%), public health news (61.9%), and political news (51.4%), while significantly higher proportions of the following types of news were regarded as awful than as nice: Environmental news (62.5%) and society news (56.5%).

4.3.2.8 Bright vs dark

There were significantly higher proportions of the following types of news that were regarded as bright than as dark: Financial news (81.8%), consumer news (80.0%), education news (75.0%), entertainment news (74.0%), science and technology news (72.9%), sports news (68.8%), other news (64.3%), commentary and opinion news (61.9%), and public health news (57.1%). On the other hand, significantly higher proportions of the following types of news were regarded as dark than as bright: Environmental news (62.5%), society news (62.0%), and political news (54.6%).

4.3.2.9 Smooth vs rough

There were significantly higher proportions of the following types of news that were perceived as smooth than as rough: Education news (100.0%), entertainment news (74.0%), science and technology news (72.9%), commentary and opinion news (71.4%), public health news (71.4%), consumer news (70.0%), financial news (63.6%), and sports news (62.5%). Significantly higher proportions of the following types of news were perceived as rough than as smooth: Society news (53.5%) and political news (45.5%). In addition, environmental news (50%) and other news (50%) were split 50/50 between smooth and rough.

4.3.2.10 Comfortable vs uncomfortable

There were significantly higher proportions of the following types of news that were perceived as comfortable than as uncomfortable: Education news (87.5%), consumer news (80.0%), science and technology news (77.1%), other news (71.4%), entertainment news (68.0%), public health news (66.7%), sports news (64.6%), commentary and opinion news (61.9%), and financial news (54.5%). Significantly higher proportions of the following types of news were perceived as uncomfortable than as comfortable: Environmental news (68.8%), society news (51.1%), and political news (51.9%).

4.3.2.11 Pleasurable vs painful

There were significantly higher proportions of the following types of news that were regarded as pleasurable than as painful: Consumer news (90.0%), education news (87.5%), financial news (81.8%), other news (78.6%), commentary and opinion news (76.2%), science and technology news (75.0%), entertainment news (72.0%), public health news (66.7%), and sports news (58.3%). On the other hand, significantly higher proportions of the following types of news were regarded as painful than as pleasurable: Society news (58.7%), environmental news (56.3%), and political news (53.0%).

4.3.3 Variations of affective reactions by demographic attributes

Compared with evaluative reactions, there were fewer demographic differences in participants' affective reactions to news. However, there were some different affective reactions to the news based on their demographic attributes. In the case of gender, a higher proportion of male participants (69.6%) viewed the news as more strong than weak than did female participants (54.3%).

Participants in different age groups also had significantly different affective reactions to the news; there were different proportions of participants who viewed news as peaceful rather than ferocious. More specifically, 88.0% of participants who were between 25 and 29 years old, 75.5% of participants who were under 20, 67.2% of participants who were 30 or above, and 59.9% of participants between 20 and 24 years old evaluated news as peaceful rather than ferocious.

There were no statistically significant differences in affective reactions to news among participants with different ethnicities, classes, or majors. There were also no significant differences in affective reactions to news between participants who are international students and American students.

4.4 Further observation of evaluative and affective reactions to news based on follow-up interviews

In our follow-up interviews, we further investigated participants' different reactions to news they recorded in their diaries. In the interviews, we asked what made them have specific evaluative and affective reactions. While analyzing the diary data, we also found that sometimes participants showed conflicting reactions to a single news item by selecting both positive and negative reactions, such as valuable and shallow. Thus, in our follow-up interviews, we also explored why they sometimes had conflicting reactions. In order to do so, we created customized interview questions for each of the 15 interviewees.

4.4.1 Further investigation of evaluative reactions to news

4.4.1.1 Deep vs shallow

On the one hand, participants stated that they evaluated news items as deep when they answered all the questions the news raised. For instance, P18 said they evaluated a news item as deep because "it sort of answers all the questions that it generates."

On the other hand, news items were often viewed as shallow when they didn't provide enough information or missed the substance. For example, P14 responded, "I don't think it actually went into the underlying issues addressing Nicaragua." News items were also evaluated as shallow when they didn't have significant implications, discussions, or meaning. For instance, P15 said, "It didn't talk about the social implications of it or it didn't really discuss why it was so great." P10 also said, "It didn't have a whole lot of meaning into it." Interestingly, one of the participants evaluated the news as shallow because "it doesn't really instigate any emotion" (P15).

4.4.1.2 Valuable vs worthless

There were various reasons why news was evaluated as valuable. The most frequently mentioned reason was intellectual benefit. More specifically, participants responded that they viewed news as valuable when they gained new information. For example, P10 said, "It was valuable for me because I learned something from it." In a similar vein, P18 responded that "This piece was valuable in the sense that it brought me some awareness, at least, of this issue." P13 also stated "When I'm reading I want to be able to learn something new." News was viewed as valuable not only when there were intellectual benefits, but also when there were emotional benefits. For instance, P18 said valuable news "either gives you more information … or makes you feel good about something." In a similar vein, P13 stated, "If something is, like, funny or entertaining to read I would say that's maybe an additional value add," which was consistent with their evaluative reaction to news that was viewed as deep or shallow.

Another similar reason to assess news as valuable was when there was substance. For example, P15 responded that they thought the news was valuable when the news "adds something substantial to your day, or to what you already know." P13 also said, "I found there was a lot of substance behind it. I remember finishing the article thinking, like, wow, that was a really worthwhile read, and I felt very content after I finished the article."

Another popular reason to view news as valuable was when the news had an impact on people or society. For example, P1 said, "For me, valuable means first it is big news … The thing that happened near us or can influence the whole world." Similarly, P27 said that valuable news "affects me or a lot of people." P40 also stated, "Stuff that has a high impact, so I think it's valuable because it's information that people should know, or maybe want to know, and it will help them in some way." Similarly, P14 responded, "For valuable, I'd definitely say if it contributes to society or if it might affect society whatever the event was, so if it affects it in the future, affects it immediately, I would say that's valuable."

News was also assessed as valuable when it was relevant to the participants. For instance, P1 said valuable news is "closely related to my campus life or personal life, like some touring information or activity information, something like that." P15 also responded that they thought a news item was valuable because it's "Good information to have if you live in Boston … makes your life better in some way."

News items were also viewed as valuable when they provided unbiased and comprehensive information (P18) or had some meaning and contributed to the discussion (P6). Interestingly, one of the participants responded that they thought the news item was valuable because it invoked memory (P18).

Contrastingly, news items were viewed as worthless when they didn't provide any new information. For instance, P13 stated, "When I meant 'worthless,' I meant, I had already known some information about this topic and so I was hoping to read the article to learn a little bit more and so I didn't really gain any new knowledge." P6 also said that they evaluated a news item as worthless because "It didn't really offer anything new. It's kind of like old news … I didn't really learn anything." In a similar vein, news items were evaluated as worthless when they didn't include useful information. During the interview, participants responded that certain news items were worthless because "it didn't offer any information on the situation" (P6) and "it doesn't really do anything to the world or society … it doesn't really contribute to anything" (P14). P31 also stated, "I would say an article that was worthless would be something that wasn't really necessary to read."

Another reason for viewing news items as worthless was when they had no direct influence on the participants. For example, P27 stated, "I don't really care if people are getting married, unless I know them." Similarly, news items viewed as worthless were "a puff piece or something that's super pop-culture-y" (P40).

Additionally, one of the participants (P1) emphasized how they evaluate news as worthless when the news is biased or untruthful.

4.4.1.3 Honest vs dishonest

On the one hand, news items were evaluated as honest when participants thought the author of the news was telling the truth (e.g., "Honest ... would be if the writer is telling the truth" (P14)), when the author's point of view is honest (e.g., "The author's point of view, I felt that they were being very honest in the article" (P31)), and when the news conveyed others' actual thoughts (e.g., "It was honest because it was saying what was going on in Texas ... what they actually thought" (P14)).

On the other hand, news items were viewed as dishonest when they had exaggerated headlines. For example, P6 responded, "The headline was kind of an exaggeration of what was happening and it kind of projected something over the story that maybe didn't quite happen but if the person does not read the story, they miss that."

4.4.1.4 Fresh vs stale

News items were viewed as fresh when they provided new information. For instance, P43 said, "It was fresh in the topic, but fresh as in, some of the information is new, so it's bringing something new to the table." This was similar to the reason for assessing news as valuable.

The same participant viewed another news item as stale "because there's already been articles about this before." In this case, news was evaluated as stale because the topic was not new.

4.4.1.5 Fair vs unfair

There were two different cases for evaluating news items as unfair. More specifically, news items were viewed as unfair when the viewpoint of the news was not fair. For example, P14 responded, "I don't think their views that they showed were fair to what was actually occurring. So I put unfair for that." In another case, a news item was viewed as unfair when the content of the news was unfair. For instance, P31 stated, "I thought that everything really going on, with that was unfair, the situation was unfair." This showed that some of the participants' reactions were sometimes about the writer/viewpoint of the news, and other times they were about the story/content of the news.

4.4.1.6 Beneficial vs harmful

There was one case in which the participant explained why they had evaluated a news item as beneficial. In this case, the participant viewed the news item as beneficial because it provided useful information. For example, the participant said, “So, it’s beneficial in the sense that they informed me about the world, or something, um, and you know, I think people need to know about these things” (P18).

4.4.1.7 Beautiful vs ugly

We asked a participant why they evaluated a news item as ugly. The participant responded, “I would just say that was more towards Trump and his actions. I would say that a lot of his actions are ugly or bad” (P31), which showed that the participant’s reaction was about the story/content of the news.

4.4.1.8 Good vs bad

On the one hand, news was viewed as good when it was credible. For instance, when asked why they evaluated a news item as good, P50 said, “I only like to read news articles that are credible, so, I guess, that’s what I kind of meant by ‘good’ or if, um, they make sense, you know what I mean? Like, if they’re well-constructed arguments and stuff.” On the other hand, news items were evaluated as bad when they were biased or untruthful. For example, P50 stated,

> Like, something that’s really, um, like, biased, or if it’s one of those. Or if I saw that it came from one of those, like, super partisan Facebook pages, like, I would count that as “bad” because that’s usually not very true stuff.

4.4.2 Further investigation of affective reactions to news

4.4.2.1 Strong vs weak

Strong reactions to news items often had to do with the size of the participants’ emotions. More specifically, participants chose strong as their reaction when they had either extremely negative or positive feelings toward news. For instance, P13's reaction to certain news items was strong because they had very negative feelings toward them. P13 stated,

> I have strong emotional reactions it's typically negative so the hot air balloon crash, um, the scandal regarding the heads of the D.N.C., and then also, um, Trump's support for Putin, that was all pretty much disgust or just, I can't believe this happened, why would something like this happen.

The same participant had a strong reaction to another news item because they had strongly positive feelings toward the news. The participant said,

> I found there was a lot of substance behind it. I remember finishing the article thinking, like, wow, that was a really worthwhile read, and I felt very content after I finished the article. So that's why I labelled that also as a strong emotional response, but typically it's not a positive one.

Another participant responded that a certain news item was strong because "it was very, very biased article yet it seemed- it was definitely trying to push an agenda" (P10). In this case, the reason for having a strong reaction was less about the negative or positive emotions but more about the voice in the news article, which was biased and pushy.

Weak reactions were not necessarily related to the size of participants' emotions or the voice of the writer of the news. Rather, they were related to the content. More specifically, a news item was viewed as weak when it didn't provide enough information. For instance, one of the participants said they marked a news item as weak because

> I didn't feel like I got the whole story, um, or the-the whole depth of the story … I just felt like I didn't, um, I didn't gain a lot from it … I didn't feel, uh, satisfied, um, and-and it left me wondering about, you know, things.
>
> (P18)

4.4.2.2 Calm vs agitated

Participants responded that they selected calm as their emotional reaction when the news items were not directly related to them or when the news didn't surprise them. For example, P21 said,

> I was calm because – I mean I'm sure I would have said something different if it were someone I know who was killed playing Pokemon Go but I mean I don't know this person personally so I didn't feel ag-and I don't play Pokemon Go, um, that would probably be another reason that I might have been agitated about it but I didn't,

showing that the participant's reaction was calm because they didn't personally know the person in the news and didn't play that game. Another participant also explained that they chose calm as their reaction "since I wasn't really surprised by some of this stuff, that Trump has said or done, I guess that would kind of cause those more calming reactions, because it didn't really faze me."

On the contrary, one of the participants said that they felt agitated when they didn't like the content of the news or others' comments on the news. The participant said, "I'm trying to stay away from Facebook because again, I just get pissed off, or agitated from people's comments on – on really just a headline" (P6). The same participant also felt agitated when there were a lot of articles that seemed unimportant. They stated, "There just seems to be a flooding of articles that are wasting space. I mean there are more important things than this kind of commentary."

4.4.2.3 Happy vs sad

In the follow-up interview, there was one case in which the participant described why they selected "sad" as their emotional reaction to news. The participant said,

> So Zika's bad, that's why I would feel sad that it spread to Florida. My family's from Brazil and I was just in Brazil in December so, when I was in Brazil, Zika was already an issue, it had been months that it had already come up, and I didn't really expect it to spread to the United States.

This shows that the participant felt sad because it was bad news that the participant didn't want to see happening.

4.4.2.4 Relaxed vs tense

There was a participant who explained why they felt tense after reading the news. The participant said, "I was tense in that this is like a serious topic that I am glad we're discussing. I was a little bit tense in that it is an important topic that needs to be discussed" (P43). The same participant also stated that they were "not relaxed about it in a way that I don't want anything to happen with it." This indicates that the participant felt tense when the topic was serious/important and also when they didn't want it to be happening.

4.4.2.5 Bright vs dark

One of the participants explained why their reaction to a certain news item was bright and to other news items was dark. In the case of the bright reaction, the participant felt bright because they appreciated the action that was delineated in the news. More specifically, the participant stated, "I appreciated that Mike Pence was willing, I guess, to diverge from Donald Trump in terms of who he was willing to support. I appreciated that move from Pence" (P13).

The same participant responded that they felt dark when they didn't agree with the action described in the news or when they were anxious about what will happen in the future. For instance, P13 said, "When I read into the article and I see, 'wow, you know, Trump has done something that I really fundamentally disagree with' and he potentially could be our next president and shape American policy, that makes me worried." In a similar vein, the participant felt dark when the news reminded them about a fact that they are not happy about. For example, P13 stated,

> Even if I read something about Donald Trump, like, Trump will praise Putin or Trump does this, or Trump supporters don't care about this or that, it makes me not feel good knowing that he has won the nomination and is a candidate for the presidency.

Another reason for feeling dark was because the content of the news was about an accident/human tragedy. More specifically, the participant said, "The hot air balloon one was just … there were a lot of mishaps in terms of safety and so I think that there was a pretty big loss of lives that could have been avoided."

4.4.3 Further investigation of conflicting reactions to news

4.4.3.1 Valuable vs shallow

Participants sometimes chose both positive and negative reactions to a single news item in their diary entries. One of the examples was selecting both valuable and shallow as their reactions to a news item. More specifically, our interview showed that participants had positive reactions because the news items provided some good information, but at the same time, they had a negative reaction because they thought the information was not impactful or not enough. For instance, P15 said,

> What I was thinking when I said this one was valuable was that this is good information to have if you live in Boston … But shallow in the sense that it doesn't really instigate any emotion. It's not deep in any way, not important, not impactful.

Similarly, P18 responded,

> This piece was valuable in the sense that it brought me some awareness, at least, of this issue. So, uh, you know, before I read-uh, listened to this clip, I didn't know anything about Kenyan schools, nor did I, like, ever think about it, right? So, uh, you know, pick out some key words at least to look into this issue a bit more if I even wanted to. So, in that sense it's valuable … I didn't feel like I got the whole story, um, or the-the whole depth of the story … I just felt like I didn't, um, I didn't gain a lot from it. Like I-I understood a few things about the cause for the burning of the schools, um, but I felt like I didn't understand the whole background of it, you know? ... So, in that sense I didn't feel, uh, satisfied, um and-and it left me wondering about, you know, things.

In other words, participants found the information they learned from the news valuable but felt that it didn't have much substance or that more information is needed.

4.4.3.2 Beneficial vs ugly

There were also multiple participants who chose both beneficial and ugly as their reactions to a news item. We asked participants why they had this conflicting reaction and found that often they had a positive reaction to the existence of the news (i.e., beneficial) and a negative reaction to the content of the news (i.e., ugly). More specifically, P18 stated,

> So, it's beneficial in the sense that they informed me about the world, or something, um, and you know, I think people need to know about these things ... maybe the ugly part is more-more of an emotional response but the article itself is not, like, written poorly or anything, I think ... But rather it, uh-it-it stimulated some ugly feelings.

In a similar vein, P10 responded,

> Well, it's important for people to understand what's going on in the gaming community ... and it's important to realize that things that we say, whether it be in a game or in real life, it has real life consequences. And this person made a threatening thing on this game and he was punished for it. So, it's really unfortunate that people do these things and that's why I think it's ugly, because this person was threatening to hurt others and that's not good, but it's good to shed light on these things so people know that these issues are there and we can learn from it.

P21 also said, "I think it's beneficial for other people to know it ... and I think it's the content that's ugly in this case."

4.4.3.3 Beautiful vs harmful

In some cases, participants selected beautiful and harmful as their reactions to the same news. When we asked why they had these conflicting reactions, P21 responded,

> It's harmful in that, I mean, the guy-in addition to, um, attacking the police car he maybe attacked someone else, like a civilian, or some-there was another part to that story so that's what I was referring to as harmful. Like, his actions were harmful ... Um, and, then, uh, as far as beautiful, I'm a huge Batman fan and I just thought that it looked kind of hilarious and the headline was hilarious.

Another participant said, "For harmful, that's definitely vice president with wife and husband, that's not good. I put beautiful because it's like House of Cards-esque and it's at least on House of Cards there was a really good political maneuver" (P14). Thus, we found that participants chose harmful because of the overall content of the news, but thought the news was beautiful because of a specific/certain aspect of the news such as hilarious title or good political maneuver depicted in the news.

4.4.3.4 Fresh vs dull

There was a participant who selected both fresh and dull as their reactions to a single news item. At the interview, the participant explained,

> I thought that was fresh because it had a lot of people's, a lot of public's reaction, and opinions that are all new and hadn't been heard of before but it was also a little bit dull because Trump is such a figure in the news, in our society right now that it's like, that's all everyone's talking about.
>
> (P43)

It seemed the participant felt the news was fresh because the opinions included in the news were new to the participant. However, the participant felt dull because the topic of the news was common.

4.4.3.5 Honest vs unfair

We had a participant who assessed the news as both honest and unfair. At the interview, the participant explained that they chose honest because the news shared others' real thoughts. However, the participant also chose unfair because they thought the opinions of people in the news were unfair and biased. More specifically, the participant said, "I don't think their views that they showed were fair to what was actually occurring. So I put unfair for that" (P14). In this case, the participant felt that the news was written in a transparent way, but that the views of people depicted in the news were unfair.

4.4.3.6 Good vs unpleasant

One of the participants chose a positive evaluative reaction and negative affective reaction to the same news. More specifically, they chose good and unpleasant as their reactions to the same news. When we asked why, the participant said,

> The Black Lives Matter Movement, sometimes it would be "oh, like, this is good news for the movement," but this is generally a dark subject so I didn't know how to answer some of those questions where it was like, "pleasant" or "unpleasant." That kind of thing.
>
> (P15)

This showed that the participant felt good about the news itself but the context made the participant feel unpleasant.

4.4.3.7 Pleasurable vs uncomfortable

When there were conflicting reactions, often they were evaluative reactions. However, there was a case when the participant had conflicting affective reactions. More specifically, P50 expressed that they felt pleasurable and uncomfortable in reaction to a single news item. At the interview, the participant shared that they felt the news was pleasurable because it was funny and relatable but felt uncomfortable at the same time because the news was self-realizing. The participant said,

> I really enjoyed Reductress articles cause they're like – I always think they're really funny. But they also, um, you know, like, are self-realizing. Oh, so I thought those were funny because it's relatable. But I'm also like "Dang it. That's me."

4.4.3.7 Sets of conflicting reactions

There were cases when participants selected a set of conflicting reactions to a single news item. In this case, their reactions were often affective rather than evaluative. For instance, P26 selected a set of positive reactions including calm, comfortable, nice, pleasant, and relaxed, then selected multiple negative reactions for the same news item, including ferocious and sad. When we asked why the participant had these conflicting affective reactions, the participant said,

> pleasant emotions were a cause from "I'm glad," like, being happy that the article is being written and that it was an article. Um, and just like-and I guess the sadness and the, um, the-the bad or negative, the other contradictory emotions came from what the actual article said, and kind of, like, relating to what the article said about the struggles of women and all that. So I think that was where the negative emotions came from.

In this case, as in other cases, the participant had positive reactions because of the existence of the news but had negative reactions because of the content of the news. In a similar vein, P21, who selected a set of positive reactions (calm, happy, nice, peaceful, and relaxed) as well as a set of negative reactions (bad, dark, unpleasant), stated that

> I'm not happy that it happened but I think I even explain, "but on the other hand if it stops people from playing it so much …" it's not – I don't think that excuses him being killed, but I'm just saying, if it makes somebody think twice, then okay.

Interestingly, P27, who selected beautiful, calm, peaceful, and relaxed as well as bad, sad, unpleasant, and weak, explained that they had positive reactions because they liked how the event was taken care of but at the same time had negative reactions because of the event itself. More specifically, P27 said,

> So, it was this scam in Miami, which, you know, is obviously bad, right? ... I thought it was, I think beautiful was in the sense that it was, like, uh, good that they got it, you know? So, I mean, it was, like, sad that, um … so it was sad that there was a scam

> in a way that people were affected poorly or negatively, but it was beautiful in the sense that, you know, "oh, great, they got broken up" … So, it was sort of a mixture of "oh, this exists, this bad thing exists" but also "oh good, but it's gone now."

This time, both positive and negative reactions were related to the content of the news, i.e., the event depicted in the news showing that one event can provoke mixed reactions. Similarly, P43 also had both positive (calm, pleasant, happy, and peaceful) and negative (weak and tense) reactions to the same news item because of the event described in the news. P43 said,

> My emotional reaction was weak because I did not get overly emotional about it. Likely I calmly agree with everything that was happening. I am calm about it but calm probably in a way that, or not released about it in a way that I don't want anything to happen with it. I was tense in that this is like a serious topic.

P31 also had both positive (pleasurable) and negative (bad, ugly) reactions because of the event described in the news. P31 explained,

> Since I wasn't really surprised by some of this stuff, that Trump has said or done, I guess that would kind of cause those more calming reactions, because it didn't really faze me. In terms of the bad or the ugly ones, I would just say that was more towards Trump and his actions.

These results indicated that people could have seemingly conflicting evaluative and affective reactions to news. In other words, they can have both positive and negative reactions when they consume news. Our in-depth interviews with the participants revealed that this was because they had different reactions to the existence, content, or context of the news. In some cases, they also had mixed reactions to the different aspects of the content of the news.

4.5 Summary

This chapter describes participants' evaluative and affective reactions to news. In particular, we report participants' evaluative and affective reactions to news we captured by using 23 semantic pairs in the diary study. This includes how these reactions differed based on types of news as well as participants' demographics such as gender, age group, ethnicity, or majors. In addition, we provide detailed information about why participants had different reactions to news, including some conflicting reactions that were further investigated in our follow-up interviews. This chapter provides a granular and in-depth analysis of participants' evaluative and affective reactions to news.

References

Ajzen, I., & Timkoe, C. (1986). Correspondence between health attitudes and behavior. *Basic and Applied Social Psychology, 7*(4), 259–276. https://doi.org/10.1207/s15324834basp0704_2

Osgood, C. E., Suci, G. J., & Tannenbaum, P. H. (1957). *The measurement of meaning.* Champaign, IL: University of Illinois Press.

Purcell, K., Rainie, L., Mitchell, A., & Rosenstiel, T. (2010). Understanding the participatory news consumer: How internet and cell phone users have turned news into a social experience. www.pewresearch.org/internet/2010/03/01/understanding-the-participatory-news-consumer/

Scott, W. E. (1967). The development of semantic differential scales as measures of "morale." *Personnel Psychology, 20*(2), 179–198. https://doi.org/10.1111/j.1744-6570.1967.tb02278.x

Tang, R., Ng, K. B., Strzalkowski, T., & Kantor, P. B. (2003). Toward machine understanding of information quality. *Proceedings of the American Society for Information Science and Technology, 40*(1), 213–220. https://doi.org/10.1002/meet.1450400127

Verhagen, T., B., van den Hooff, & Meents, S. (2015). Toward a better use of the semantic differential in IS research: An integrative framework of suggested action. *Journal of the Association for Information Systems, 16*(2), 108–143. https://aisel.aisnet.org/jais/vol16/iss2/1/

5 Summary and Conclusion

5.1 Overview

In previous chapters, we described the key findings from a series of studies that we conducted on mobile news information behavior. Through detailed accounts of participants' news consumption activities, including noticing/receiving, reading, finding, sharing, and storing news on their mobile devices, as well as their evaluative and emotional reactions to the news consumed through their smartphones, we discovered the key patterns and characteristics associated with news consumption on mobile platforms.

In this chapter, we discuss the impact of mobile news consumption on individual users' mobile activities, social behaviors, political interactions, and community engagement. In addition, we make recommendations for improvements in mobile devices and news app design based on our findings. We end this chapter with a discussion of further areas of exploration and examination of the subject matter.

5.2 Impact on mobile activities, social behavior, and political/community engagement

Our findings show that mobile devices, including smartphones, have become an indispensable part of people's daily life. This is consistent with existing research. As pointed out by Ahonen (2013), mobile is the seventh mass medium following print, recordings, cinema, radio, television, and internet, and it is the first truly personalized mass medium. Mobile technology has ultimately changed the landscape of news consumption and transformed the

DOI: 10.4324/9781003053002-5

ecology of mass media. Li (2014) suggested that mobile phones now work as "a functional channel to deliver news information" (p. 298). According to multiple research studies (Purcell et al., 2010; O'Brien & Freund, 2014; Struckmann & Karnowski, 2016), users' relationships to news have changed as news is now not only pocket-sized and personalized, but the consumption of news has also become a socially engaging, socially driven, and participatory activity. Back in 2010, researchers (Purcell et al., 2010) from the Pew Research Center observed that "people's relationship to news is becoming portable, personalized, and participatory" (p. 2). Purcell et al. (2010) further indicate that

> To a great extent, people's experience of news, especially on the internet, is becoming a shared social experience as people swap links in emails, post news stories on their social networking site feeds, highlight news stories in their Tweets, and haggle over the meaning of events in discussion threads. For instance, more than 8 in 10 online news consumers get or share links in emails. (p. 2)

Lu and Holocome (2016) observed that among online news consumers, there has been a striking increase in mobile audience and a continuing shift to mobile devices. Not only have mobile devices provided their users a means to keep abreast of current social and political happenings, but the general public has also been empowered to exchange information in a real-time manner and share opinions and reactions about certain societal dynamics and political activities through private direct messages or publicly viewable comments. The specific enabling features of engaged mobile news participation include ubiquity, constant connectivity, instant interactivity, and personalization (Martin, 2014). In terms of personalization, Cunningham, Nichols, Hinze, and Bowen (2016) explored the news behavior of 35 undergraduate students and argued that students seemed to rely more on non-traditional news sources than conventional broadcast news because they desired "a more personalized news information feed" (p. 265).

The findings of our studies, similar to previous findings, revealed that mobile news consumption has become part of day-to-day news consumption for university students. Students not only used their smartphones to notice, receive, read, find, share, and store news on a daily basis, but they also were very engaged and actively participating in exchanging, sharing, commenting on, and discussing news with different circles of people in their lives. We discovered that there were demographic differences including gender, age group, ethnicity, school, class level, student type, and major in a variety of news consumption activities, and we also found that people did have reactions to or emotional connections with the news stories that they were consuming.

Through purposive sampling and a pre-diary survey, a diary study method, and a follow-up interviews to collect data, our research revealed a rich dimension of university students' mobile consumption activities and their near real-time reactions to news. The conceptual and scholarly contribution of this research study is that it broadens and deepens our understanding of mobile information behavior. Our diary data revealed how university students in the United States consume news on their mobile phones, highlighting their focus on political news, including election news, and their reliance on news apps or social media to read, find, and share news. Using a diary tool allowed us to not only obtain details about each news story that a participant submitted, but also to capture specific activity streams that the participant went through as they consumed the news (e.g., reading, finding, sharing, and storing), and their evaluative and affective reactions to each news story they submitted. Such richness in the behavior details makes the diary method empirically effective and solid. In addition, analysis of the 15 interview responses enables a more accurate and enriched understanding of participants' selections of adjective terms and how they associated those terms with various types of news. In the sections below, we will provide some examples of the various sorts of news captured by our participants to demonstrate how mobile news consumption has become a primary method of daily news consumption for university students.

5.2.1 Political and society news examples

As previously stated before, our participants paid great attention to political and society news. These were, proportionately, the two most common news types (35% and 18%, respectively); they occupied close to 45% of all the news types consumed. Political news was very closely tied to the upcoming 2016 presidential election

Figure 5.1 Muslim Women Call out Donald Trump.

in the United States. Figures 5.1, 5.2, 5.3, and 5.4 show how the various news items, including political and society news, were captured by our study participants. These images revealed that the university students cared a lot about the world, their society and communities, as well as what was happening in the election. News consumed via their mobile phones was their primary source of information.

5.2.2 *Entertainment news examples*

As college students, our study participants also enjoyed receiving, reading, and sharing entertainment news. Entertainment news was the third most popular type of news (10%) among our study participants. In the following screenshots captured by our participants, we can see that the participants' interests ranged from games (Figure 5.5) to cartoons (Figure 5.6) to celebrity feuds (Figure 5.7).

Europe

Munich shooting: Police hunt 'attackers'

24 minutes ago Europe

AFP

There is a big police presence at the shopping centre

Police in the German city of Munich say the perpetrators of a shooting attack are still on the run, and they advise people to avoid public places.

There are reports of at least six people killed, but police have not confirmed that figure.

Figure 5.2 Munich Shooting News.

SHARE

OBSERVER

OPINION

Wikileaks Proves Primary Was Rigged: DNC Undermined Democracy

20,000 freshly leaked emails reveal resentful disdain toward Sanders, as party favored Clinton long before any votes were cast

BY MICHAEL SAINATO
JULY 22, 2016 11:00 AM

Figure 5.3 Wikileaks and Sanders versus Clinton.

Figure 5.4 The Racist History of Portland.

Figure 5.5 Pokémon Sun and Moon Game.

Figure 5.6 Netflix's "Little Witch Academia" Trailer.

Figure 5.7 Feud between Taylor Swift and Kim Kardashian/Kanye West.

5.2.3 *Sports news examples*

Among all news types consumed, close to 10% of the news stories submitted were sports news. Note that during the first round of data collection, the Rio 2016 Summer Olympics were going on. Many participants paid attention to the Olympics, such as record-breaking performances by US athletes (Figure 5.8) or the events surrounding the games (Figures 5.9–5.11). There were also other sports news people paid attention to, for instance, in Figure 5.12, the news was about an extreme sport.

5.2.4 *Science/technology news examples*

Among all the news stories submitted, 9% were science/technology news. Given that our participants were university students, it is not surprising that they were interested in the advancement of science and technology. Among our diary participants, close to 40% of

Figure 5.8 Katie Ledecky Broke the World Record and Got the First Gold Medal for the United States.

Figure 5.9 Russian Team Banned from Olympics.

Figure 5.10 Ramp for Competitors' Boats Collapsed.

Figure 5.11 Australia Refused to Move Their Team to the Olympic Village.

Figure 5.12 Skydiver with No Parachute.

Figure 5.13 Europe's First Mars Rover.

the participants majored in science (31.4%) and engineering (7.8%). As shown in Figures 5.13–5.15, the science/technology news that our participants paid attention to varied from aerospace technology (Figure 5.13) to solar-powered airplane technology (Figure 5.14), oceanography (Figure 5.15), and smartphone technology (Figure 5.16).

5.2.5 *Public health or health news examples*

Another type of news that our participants read about on their mobile phones was health-related or public-health news. Four percent of the news stories submitted were health-related. These stories varied from the Zika virus (Figures 5.17 and 5.18) to heart health (Figure 5.19) and mental health issues (Figure 5.20). These stories show that university students in the United States care about a broad spectrum of human health issues, ranging from general public health threats to specific health concerns.

Figure 5.14 Solar-powered Plane.

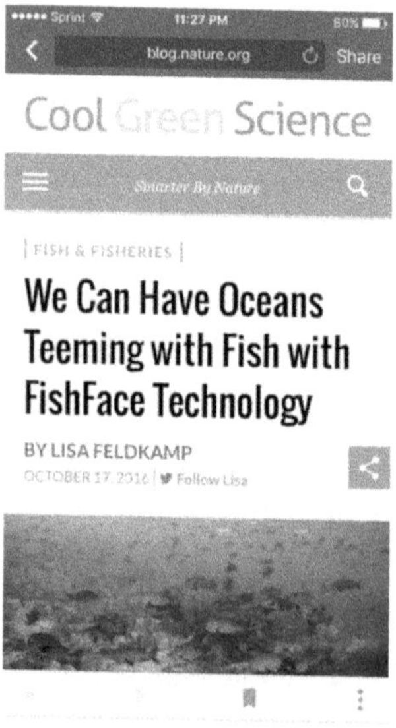

Figure 5.15 FishFace Technology.

Figure 5.16 Smartphone Technology.

Figure 5.17 Zika Virus.

Figure 5.18 Zika Virus and Impact on Pregnant Women.

Figure 5.19 Deep Space and Heart Problems.

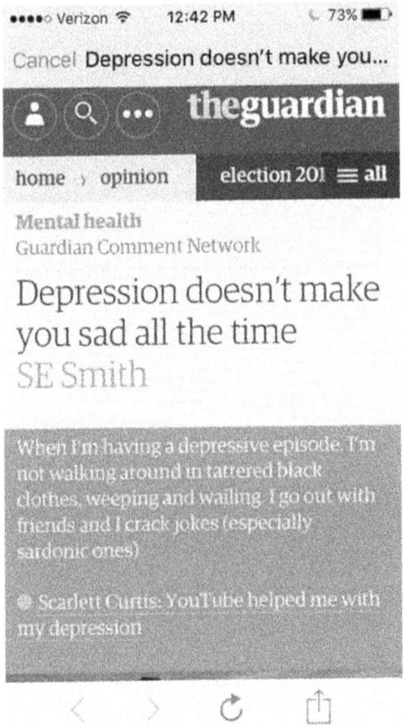

Figure 5.20 Depression and Sadness.

5.2.6 Other types of news examples

A variety of other types of news were submitted by participants, which demonstrates that consuming news on mobile devices has become a normal activity in their daily lives. This includes business and finance news (Figure 5.21), weight loss advice (Figure 5.22), and advice on friends (Figure 5.23).

Figure 5.21 Yahoo to Sell Web Business to Verizon.

Figure 5.22 More Is Better: Fitness Advice.

SHARE

The New York Times

NEWS ANALYSIS

Do Your Friends Actually Like You?

BY KATE MURPHY
AUGUST 6, 2016

THINK of all the people with whom you interact during the course of a day, week, month and year. The many souls with whom you might exchange a greeting or give a warm embrace; engage in chitchat or have a deeper conversation. All those who, by some accident of fate, inhabit your world.

Figure 5.23 Friends and You.

5.3 Recommendations on mobile device and news app design

As revealed in earlier chapters and sections, mobile news consumption is a routine part of daily life for university students. Our results also showed that news apps were used by our participants as their main source of news, and the younger the participants' age group, the higher the percentage of participants who used news apps as their primary channel of consuming news. There was still variation in terms of news app features and functionality, which impacted the extent of use and the quality of user experience.

The following are the key areas of recommendations we make based on our conversations with our study participants:

Recommendation 1. Enable seamless operation for reading, searching, sharing, and storing news stories

We observed that when consuming news via their mobile phones, people carried out multiple activities in one sitting. This means that mobile news apps need to be designed in a manner that supports seamless transitions from one sequence to another. When people are reading a news story, they might then search for more comprehensive coverage of the same news. Then, when they want to share a segment of the news or the entirety of the news story, they should be easily able to do that. If they wish to save the story, they should also be able to do so painlessly. Furthermore, if they want to return to the story and repeat some of the activities, they should be able to do that without getting lost.

Recommendation 2. Enhance sharing and storing functionality

Our participants utilize the sharing feature quite extensively, but the capability of news apps to enable sharing with different levels of detail or multimedia elements needs to be strengthened. Currently, people simply make do; for example, they might just do a screen capture and send the image to their friends/family or other recipients via email. To support news sharing and enable news sharing as a collective and interactive experience, mobile news app designers might create some features to allow users to share specific sections or objects of the news stories without leaving the app.

For storing news, most of the news apps do not support more advanced storage capabilities. This prevented our participants from using the "news storing" activity frequently. If the activity of "storing/saving the news items" can be enhanced by linking to a cloud-based account where users can easily access and share saved news items when needed, that would make the storing activity an enjoyable and useful experience, and people would use it. Currently, such a feature is mostly not supported or very clunky for people to use. Because of the difficulty in storing/saving news items through mobile apps, people ended up not carrying out that activity in their news consumption process.

Recommendation 3. Support various formats of news

Our participants utilized all kinds of news formats, including text, image, video, etc. However, some of the images or videos may not be adapted to the mobile screen, restricting users' enjoyment of the news items to what they can see or view fully. News app designers should consider multiple ways to enhance the effective delivery of their multimedia content. When linking to multimedia players for videos, users should be able to easily return to the original news story.

5.4 Further areas of exploration and examination

In this study, participants were undergraduate and graduate students in the United States. They are active users of smartphones, so they were considered a good population for the study. However, our investigations were limited to this specific population. It will be interesting to extend the study by including other populations, such as the general public, and explore their smartphone news consumption behavior. This would allow us to further investigate demographic differences and have a more comprehensive understanding of mobile news consumption behavior. We can also expand the study by examining smartphone users in different countries and investigating cultural differences in smartphone news consumption behaviors.

This study focused on the characteristics of news consumed by participants via their mobile phones, different news consumption activities, and their various reactions to mobile news. The findings provide an in-depth understanding of mobile news consumption behavior. However, this study did not focus much on the practical aspects of mobile news consumption. In future studies, it will be worthwhile to identify any challenges people experience while consuming news via their mobile devices so that the findings can inform designers in developing tools and applications that better support smartphone users' news consumption activities.

5.5 Summary

In this chapter, we shared some details about the various types of news that our study participants were interested in to demonstrate how news consumption through smart phones has become a daily news consumption activity in university students' lives. With mobile devices and news apps altering the news consumption landscape by enabling users' active participation in news sharing, commenting, activism, and building connections, the significance of such activities should not be underestimated. Based on what we learned from our study participants, we presented recommendations for designers of news apps or news sites to make the mobile news consumption a user friendly and seamless experience.

References

Ahonen, T. (2013). Mobile and megatrends. In P. A. Bruck & M. Rao (eds.), *Going mobile: Applications and innovations for the worldwide mobile ecosystem* (pp. 29–45). Medford, NJ: Information Today.

Cunningham, S., Nichols, D., Hinze, A., & Bowen, J. (2016). What's news? Encounters with news in everyday life: A study of behaviours and attitudes. *International Journal on Digital Libraries, 17*(3), 257–271.

Li, X. (2014). Technology facility and news affinity: Predictors of using mobile phones as a news device. In X. Xu (ed.), *Interdisciplinary mobile media and communications: Social, political, and economic implications* (pp. 278–304). IGI Global, Hershey, Pennsylvania, USA.

Lu, K., & Holco mb, J. (2016). Digital news – Audience: Fact sheet. In A. Mitchell, J. Holcomb, & R. Weasel (eds.), *State of the News Media 2016* (pp. 44–59). https://search.issuelab.org/resource/state-of-the-news-media-2016-digital-news-audience-fact-sheet.html

Martin, J. A. (2014). Mobile media and political participation: Defining and developing an emerging field. *Mobile Media & Communication 2*(2), 173–195.

O'Brien, H., Freund, L., & Westman, S. (2014). What motivates the online news browser? News item selection in a social information seeking scenario. *Information Research, 19*(3), www.informationr.net/ir/19-3/paper634.html#.V8ssaFQrKM8 (accessed December 2022).

Purcell, K., Rainie, L., Mitchell, A., Rosenstiel, T., & Olmstead, K. (2010). Understanding the participatory news consumer: How internet and cell phone users have turned news into a social experience. Report, Pew Research Center, Washington, D. C.

Struckmann, S., & Karnowski, V. (2016). News consumption in a changing media ecology: An MESM-study on mobile news. *Telematics and Informatics, 33*(2), 309–319.

Index

Note: Page locators in **bold** and *italics* represents tables and figures, respectively.

affective reactions, to news: based on follow-up interviews 92–105; bipolar adjective pairs for 80, **81**; bright *vs* dark 90, 99–100; calm *vs* agitated 88–9, 98; comfortable *vs* uncomfortable 91; happy *vs* sad 89, 98–9; nice *vs* awful 90; peaceful *vs* ferocious 89; pleasant *vs* unpleasant 89; pleasurable *vs* painful 91; positive and negative reactions 87–8; relaxed *vs* tense 90, 99; smooth *vs* rough 90–1; strong *vs* weak 88, 96–7; variations by demographic attributes 91–2; variations by types of news 88–91

background-oriented digital news consumer 4
Black Lives Matter Movement 103
bookmarking 71–5

commentary and opinion news 82, 83, 84, 88–91
conflicting reactions to news, investigation of: beautiful *vs* harmful 101–2; beneficial *vs* ugly 101; fresh *vs* dull 102; good *vs* unpleasant 103; honest *vs* unfair 102–3; pleasurable *vs* uncomfortable 103; sets of 104–5; valuable *vs* shallow 100–1
consumer news 82, 83, 88–91
copying and pasting, the news story 71–2
crime news 16

data collection 9, 11, 114
demographic differences, in news consumption: demographics and the types of news 21–4; sources of news 24–7, 27–9
depression and sadness *121*
digital news consumers 4, 6, 18
digital news media, emergence of 4
Digital News Report 2019 1

education news 82, 83, 88–91
empirical studies, on mobile news consumption 3–8; in historical and political context 8–9; news consumer typology 4–6; news consumption frameworks 4–6; use of mobile news services 6–8
entertainment news 16, 82, 83, 88–91, 110–13

environmental news 82, 83, 84, 88–91
Europe's First Mars Rover *117*
evaluative reactions, to news: based on follow-up interviews 92–105; beautiful *vs* ugly 84, 96; beneficial *vs* harmful 84, 96; bipolar adjective pairs for 80, **80**; deep *vs* shallow 82, 92–3; fair *vs* unfair 95–6; fresh *vs* stale 83, 95; good *vs* bad 84, 96; heavy *vs* light 82–3; honest *vs* dishonest 83, 95; sharp *vs* dull 83; valuable *vs* worthless 82, 93–5; variations by demographic attributes 84–7; variations by types of news 81–4; wide–narrow semantic differential pair for analysing 81
extent of news sharing: by age groups 62–3; demographic differences in 62–3; by ethnic group 63; overview of 61–2; by student type 63

Facebook 18, 36, 56, 67–8
fake news, news reporting from 26
financial news 82, 83, 84, 88–91
finding news 46–50; additional insights about 55–7; class types 50, 53–4; demographic differences in 49–50; in different age groups 50, 51; in different ethnic group 52–3; in different majors 50, 54–5; gender differences in 49–50; methods of 50–5; news finding behavior 49–50; reasons for 56–7; student types 50
FishFace Technology *118*
FlexMR (mobile diary app) 10
follow-up interviews, reactions to news based on 92–105; affective reactions to news 96–100; evaluative reactions to news 92–6; investigation of conflicting reactions to news 100–5
format of news 19–21; demographic differences in 27–9; top three formats **27**, **28**, **29**

Gen Z news users 1
Google search 19, 25, 36, 52, 54

heavy newspaper reader 4

Instagram 18
instant messaging/texting 59, 61, 69
international mobility: leisure-related 8; work-related 8

Kardashian, Kim *113*

Lede (real-time blogs) 19
Ledecky, Katie *114*
light newspaper reader 4
Line Today 3

Media Online 7
Media on mobile 7
methods of finding the news 50–5; by age group 51, **51**; for all major groups 54–5, **55**; by class 53–4, **53–4**; by ethnic group **52**, 52–3
methods of reading 41–4, **44**, 46; additional insights about 44–6; by age group 42–3; for all major groups 44; by class 43; demographic differences in 42–4; by ethnic group 43; overall methods 41–2
mobile device and news app design, recommendations on 123–5
mobile interfaces, transformational power of 2
mobile-native generation 2
mobile news: apps 31; characteristics of 11; reasons for reading or not reading 46
mobile news consumption: bystanders of 4; data collection methods and the timeline **9**;

defined 6; empirical studies on 3–8; frameworks of 4–6; global trends in 2–3; lifecycle of 11; news consumer typology and 4–6; research model for behavior of 11; research work on 9–11; role of mobile devices in 1–2; themes of 3–4; video news content 3
mobile news services, usage of 6–7
mobile news sharing: in Asian countries 3; in China 3; ecosystem of 2; empirical studies on 3–8; popularity of 2; social phenomenon of 2; in United Kingdom 3; of video news content 3
mobile phone news 6
mobile technology 107; advancement of 8; development of 2
multimedia presentations 20
Munich shooting news *111*

net-based media 18
net-based news 6
Netflix's "Little Witch Academia" trailer *113*
Net-Newsers 4, 18
news: app functions 2; demographics and the types of 21–4; formats of 19–21; program 7; on social events 16; on social media 19; sources of 18–19; types of 16–18; update addict 4
news app 52, 123–5
news consumers: characteristics of 4; disengaged 4; groups of 4; integrators 4; Net-Newsers 4; segments of 4; traditionalists 4; types of 4, **5–6**
news sharing, methods of 67–8; demographic differences in 58–61; by ethnic groups 60, **60**; gender differences in 59; by major groups 60–1, **61**; overview of 58; reasons for choosing 68–9
news stories, drawing people's attention: classes with regard to 38–9; gender differences 37–8; majors 39–40
New York Times (NYT) 37, 45

online news consumers 108
other news: affective reactions to 90; evaluative reactions to 82–4

people's reactions to news: bipolar adjective pairs for affective reactions 80, **81**; bipolar adjective pairs for evaluative reactions 80, **80**; method of measuring 79; use of semantic differential scales for gauging 79–80; *see also* affective reactions, to news; evaluative reactions, to news
personal blogs 67
Pew Research Center 4, 108
Pokémon Sun and Moon Game *112*
political news 82, 83, 84, 88–91, 109–10
popular culture-oriented digital news consumer 4
Portland, racist history of *112*
pre-diary online survey 10
print newspapers, news from 20
public health news: affective reactions to 88–91; evaluative reactions to 16, 82–4; examples of 117–21

qualitative Q method study 4

reading behavior, insights about 44
reading news: demographic differences in 41, 42–4; differences among school type in 41; ethnic differences in 41; gender differences in 41; majors 41; methods of 41–4; news reading behavior 40–1; participants' reading behavior in

42; reasons for using a method of **48**
reading or not reading news, common reasons for **47**
receiving/noticing news, on mobile devices 31–40; additional reasons for 36–7; age groups with regard to 33; class levels with regard to 33–4; gender differences in 32; majors or academic specializations 35; reasons for 32, **32**
regional omnivorous news consumer 4
Rio Summer Olympics (2016) 8

science and technology news 16, 82–4, 83, 88–91
screen capture, of the news story 73–4
service-based news 19
sharing news 57–69; additional insights about 64–9; by age group 57; attitude toward 64; by class 58; by ethnic group 57; extent of 61–3; methods of 58–61, 67–8; news sharing behaviors 57–8; reasons for sharing or not sharing news **65–6**, 65–7; by school types 57–8; on social media 64; by student types 58; timing of 64
SmartNews 36
smartphones: sales of 1; technology 2, *119*; use in news consumption 1–2
social media 51, 56; sharing news on 64
society news 82–4, 88–91, 109–10
solar-powered plane *118*
SOM survey 8
sources of news, demographic differences in 24–7
sports news: affective reactions to 88–91; data collection 114; evaluative reactions to 82, 83, 84; examples of 114; Rio 2016 Summer Olympics 114
storing of news 69–77; additional insights about 76–7; by age differences 71–2, **72**; by class level 74, **75**; demographic differences in 70–5; in different majors 74–5, **76**; by ethnicity 72–3, **73**; gender differences in 70–1, **71**; news storing behaviors 69–70, 76; reasons for 77; by school types 73, **74**
study participants, mobile news consumed by: demographic differences in 21–9; diary study participants 14; follow-up interview participants 16; interviewees' demographic information **17**; pre-diary survey participants 14; sources of news consumed by participants *20*; types of *18*
Swift, Taylor *113*

Television Viewing 7
Twitter 18, 36, 68

video news content, trends in sharing of 3

Web news and sports 7
WeChat 69
West, Kanye *113*
WhatsApp 69
Wikileaks and Sanders *vs* Clinton *111*

Yahoo! News 3

Zika virus outbreak (2016) 8, 117, *119*; impact on pregnant women *120*

Milton Keynes UK
Ingram Content Group UK Ltd.
UKHW022055291124
451732UK00005B/37

9 780367 512071